Cancel Culture

Other Books of Related Interest

Opposing Viewpoints Series

America's Changing Demographics
Feminism
Gender in the 21st Century
Interpreting the Bill of Rights
Toxic Masculinity

At Issue Series

Civil Disobedience
Cyberwarfare
The Federal Budget and Government Spending
Gender Politics
The Opioid Crisis

Current Controversies Series

America's Mental Health Crisis
Are There Two Americas?
Drones, Surveillance, and Targeted Killings
Enhanced Interrogation and Torture
Returning Soldiers and PTSD

> "Congress shall make no law ... abridging the freedom of speech, or of the press."

First Amendment to the US Constitution

The basic foundation of our democracy is the First Amendment guarantee of freedom of expression. The Opposing Viewpoints series is dedicated to the concept of this basic freedom and the idea that it is more important to practice it than to enshrine it.

OPPOSING
VIEWPOINTS®
SERIES

Cancel Culture

Lita Sorensen, Book Editor

GREENHAVEN
PUBLISHING

To my little sister, Toni Sorensen, 1970–2020. Being "right" does not mean winning in some absurd interpersonal competition. Winning is that thing when truth and justice align to allow all individuals the rights and means to fulfill their God-given dreams and potential as human beings and work toward happiness.

Published in 2022 by Greenhaven Publishing, LLC
353 3rd Avenue, Suite 255, New York, NY 10010

Articles in Greenhaven Publishing anthologies are often edited for length to meet page requirements. In addition, original titles of these works are changed to clearly present the main thesis and to explicitly indicate the author's opinion. Every effort is made to ensure that Greenhaven Publishing accurately reflects the original intent of the authors. Every effort has been made to trace the owners of the copyrighted material.

Cover image: RoBird/Shutterstock.com

Library of Congress Cataloging-in-Publication Data

Names: Sorensen, Lita, editor.
Title: Cancel culture / Lita Sorensen, book editor.
Description: First edition. | New York : Greenhaven Publishing, 2022. | Series: Opposing viewpoints | Includes bibliographical references and index. | Audience: Ages 15 | Audience: Grades 10–12 | Summary: "Anthology of diverse perspectives regarding the social phenomenon of cancel culture, public shaming, and mob mentality. Volume introduction, guided reading questions, introductory material, critical thinking questions, resource material and index"— Provided by publisher.
Identifiers: LCCN 2020051567 | ISBN 9781534507593 (library binding) | ISBN 9781534507579 (paperback)
Subjects: LCSH: Cancel culture. | Social pressure. | Shame. | Internet—Social aspects. | Internet and activism.
Classification: LCC HM1176 .C35 2022 | DDC 302.23/1—dc23
LC record available at https://lccn.loc.gov/2020051567

Manufactured in the United States of America

Website: http://greenhavenpublishing.com

Contents

Chapter 3: What Social Problems Does Cancel Culture Highlight?

Chapter 4: Will Cancel Culture Be Canceled?

The Importance of Opposing Viewpoints

Perhaps every generation experiences a period in time in which the populace seems especially polarized, starkly divided on the important issues of the day and gravitating toward the far ends of the political spectrum and away from a consensus-facilitating middle ground. The world that today's students are growing up in and that they will soon enter into as active and engaged citizens is deeply fragmented in just this way. Issues relating to terrorism, immigration, women's rights, minority rights, race relations, health care, taxation, wealth and poverty, the environment, policing, military intervention, the proper role of government—in some ways, perennial issues that are freshly and uniquely urgent and vital with each new generation—are currently roiling the world.

If we are to foster a knowledgeable, responsible, active, and engaged citizenry among today's youth, we must provide them with the intellectual, interpretive, and critical-thinking tools and experience necessary to make sense of the world around them and of the all-important debates and arguments that inform it. After all, the outcome of these debates will in large measure determine the future course, prospects, and outcomes of the world and its peoples, particularly its youth. If they are to become successful members of society and productive and informed citizens, students need to learn how to evaluate the strengths and weaknesses of someone else's arguments, how to sift fact from opinion and fallacy, and how to test the relative merits and validity of their own opinions against the known facts and the best possible available information. The landmark series Opposing Viewpoints has been providing students with just such critical-thinking skills and exposure to the debates surrounding society's most urgent contemporary issues for many years, and it continues to serve this essential role with undiminished commitment, care, and rigor.

The key to the series's success in achieving its goal of sharpening students' critical-thinking and analytic skills resides in its title—

Opposing Viewpoints. In every intriguing, compelling, and engaging volume of this series, readers are presented with the widest possible spectrum of distinct viewpoints, expert opinions, and informed argumentation and commentary, supplied by some of today's leading academics, thinkers, analysts, politicians, policy makers, economists, activists, change agents, and advocates. Every opinion and argument anthologized here is presented objectively and accorded respect. There is no editorializing in any introductory text or in the arrangement and order of the pieces. No piece is included as a "straw man," an easy ideological target for cheap point-scoring. As wide and inclusive a range of viewpoints as possible is offered, with no privileging of one particular political ideology or cultural perspective over another. It is left to each individual reader to evaluate the relative merits of each argument— as he or she sees it, and with the use of ever-growing critical-thinking skills—and grapple with his or her own assumptions, beliefs, and perspectives to determine how convincing or successful any given argument is and how the reader's own stance on the issue may be modified or altered in response to it.

This process is facilitated and supported by volume, chapter, and selection introductions that provide readers with the essential context they need to begin engaging with the spotlighted issues, with the debates surrounding them, and with their own perhaps shifting or nascent opinions on them. In addition, guided reading and discussion questions encourage readers to determine the authors' point of view and purpose, interrogate and analyze the various arguments and their rhetoric and structure, evaluate the arguments' strengths and weaknesses, test their claims against available facts and evidence, judge the validity of the reasoning, and bring into clearer, sharper focus the reader's own beliefs and conclusions and how they may differ from or align with those in the collection or those of their classmates.

Research has shown that reading comprehension skills improve dramatically when students are provided with compelling, intriguing, and relevant "discussable" texts. The subject matter of these collections could not be more compelling, intriguing, or urgently relevant to today's students and the world they are poised to inherit. The anthologized articles and the reading and discussion questions that are included with them also provide the basis for stimulating, lively, and passionate classroom debates. Students who are compelled to anticipate objections to their own argument and identify the flaws in those of an opponent read more carefully, think more critically, and steep themselves in relevant context, facts, and information more thoroughly. In short, using discussable text of the kind provided by every single volume in the Opposing Viewpoints series encourages close reading, facilitates reading comprehension, fosters research, strengthens critical thinking, and greatly enlivens and energizes classroom discussion and participation. The entire learning process is deepened, extended, and strengthened.

For all of these reasons, Opposing Viewpoints continues to be exactly the right resource at exactly the right time—when we most need to provide readers with the critical-thinking tools and skills that will not only serve them well in school but also in their careers and their daily lives as decision-making family members, community members, and citizens. This series encourages respectful engagement with and analysis of opposing viewpoints and fosters a resulting increase in the strength and rigor of one's own opinions and stances. As such, it helps make readers "future ready," and that readiness will pay rich dividends for the readers themselves, for the citizenry, for our society, and for the world at large.

Introduction

> *"The restriction of debate, whether by a repressive government or an intolerant society, invariably hurts those who lack power and makes everyone less capable of democratic participation. The way to defeat bad ideas is by exposure, argument, and persuasion, not by trying to silence or wish them away."*
>
> —*"A Letter on Justice and Open Debate,"* Harper's Magazine, *July 7, 2020*

Why now? Why do we find ourselves, in this particular time, living in a culture of cancellation—a modern-day, extreme version of censorship, mob mentality, and public shaming? What conditions had to be present to brew the perfect storm for people to unite, express outrage, and (sometimes) effect change?

While public shaming has occurred in societies throughout history, it wasn't until the rise of the internet and social media that it became possible for people—even those who did not traditionally have a platform—to reach a large and global audience. Spreading a message quickly is great; that is, until there is so much content that people begin forwarding articles and posts without investigating the full story behind what they're regramming or retweeting. At its best, this "hashtag activism" can inspire people and even change the world. At its worst, it promotes outrage and cruelty without the benefit of discourse.

Some of these conditions seemed to converge when Donald Trump was elected US president in 2016. Almost immediately, protests began. Throngs of women and their allies marched on the mall in Washington, DC, as well as in other cities around the world. The administration's immigration policies moved many to protest at airports. The police killing of one Black man too many catapulted the Black Lives Matter hashtag into massive, routine protests. After years of being asleep, suddenly Americans were "woke." But this woke culture had a downside: the swift and impassioned rush to punish those who dared to express unpopular opinions. For their part, the "unwoke" practiced their own form of cancellation as well, including—at the extreme—the dissemination of far-right conspiracy theories purporting to identify some celebrities and politicians on the left as pedophiles.

Our digital lives are not easy to erase, and many a public figure has been canceled for resurfaced comments made in the deep past. Corporations give in to public pressure and fire or dismiss the culprit, but this can be rectified with a sincere apology. Often, the canceled person gains sympathy and a career boost from the whole thing.

This is not to suggest that some cancellations are unwarranted. For example, the surge of the #MeToo movement as a reckoning for Hollywood mogul Harvey Weinstein effectively brought a loathsome sex abuser and rapist to justice.

But the intentions and actions behind today's cancel culture aren't always so clearly defined. Things got murky, for instance, with the Covington Catholic School Boys case in 2019, involving very short viral video clips of doubtful origin showing minors wearing red Trump MAGA hats supposedly confronting Native American activists. The videos and interpretations of what actually happened polarized Americans, with the anger initially settling on the Covington students, resulting in death threats from enraged internet citizens and multi-million-dollar lawsuits.

Many observers thought they "knew" what happened and vented their anger on the young students, some actually vowing publicly that they would contact the boys' school and recommend expulsion. Of course, even if this action was well-meaning toward principles of respect or fairness, other fundamentals in the situation come into play, such as the MAGA hat offenders being young minors, standing laws and statutes regarding defamation and libel, and the right to a presumed innocence before community vigilantism.

There are many interpretations of what cancel culture actually is and even thoughts on whether it actually exists. There are ideas on its nature coming from all realms of the political spectrum. The *New York Times* ran a series of theses by various authors on the subject. *Harper's Magazine* published an open letter in July 2020 on justice and open debate, imploring a toleration of differences in lieu of ideological conformity and signed by preeminent intellectuals, writers, and scholars, some of whom have found themselves the objects of cancellation.

Perhaps the best definition found was included in the *Harper's Magazine* group letter. In their writing, the scholars and intellectuals, among them people as diverse as Noam Chomsky and J. K. Rowling, stated that cancel culture is a sort of "illiberalism," or a seeming belief by some members on the left of the political spectrum given forces of authoritarianism threatening our society that there must necessarily be a choice between justice and freedom of expression. The writers go on to state that this is a false choice, as truly one ideal cannot exist without the other. The writers call for tolerance and openness in society without fear of professional or personal reprisal as the antidote.

The diverse array of perspectives in *Opposing Viewpoints: Cancel Culture* confront this complex issue as it pertains to our society today. In chapters titled "What Is Cancel Culture?," "How Does Cancel Culture Affect Us?," "What Social Problems Does Cancel Culture Highlight?," and "Will Cancel Culture Be Canceled?," viewpoint authors address a phenomenon that is certainly not new but has taken on different characteristics and consequences in this digital age.

OPPOSING
VIEWPOINTS®
SERIES

CHAPTER 1

What Is
Cancel Culture?

Chapter Preface

To some extent, public shaming and ostracization as a consequence of perceived bad behavior has existed throughout history. But the term *cancel culture* was only popularized around 2017, when movements like #MeToo came into existence via Twitter, and celebrities and other powerful people were increasingly being held accountable for objectionable behavior and actions. Lisa Nakamura, a professor and researcher based at the University of Michigan who studies race, gender, and sexuality and how it connects to online usage, told the *New York Times* in 2018 that a cancellation was a "cultural boycott" of a certain celebrity, brand, company, or concept.

But that is just one side of the spectrum of what cancel culture can be. As time has gone on, less well-known figures and ordinary people have faced often overly critical actions taken against them that have affected their careers or personal lives for relatively minor errors or differences of opinion.

Many people now recognize cancel culture as a negative movement; still others insist cancel culture doesn't actually exist. Recently, the term has been politicized, especially taken on by the political right and eventually by former president Donald Trump, who criticized it during his term in office as a leftist phenomenon in an attempt to rile up his supporters. On the other side, former president Barack Obama gained widespread approval from both conservatives and liberals alike when he recognized the trend as negative and not true activism.

The *Insider* notes that Google Trends data shows there was nearly nonexistent search interest in the phrase "cancel culture" until the second half of 2018 and early 2019. The most interest came in July of 2020, along with a spew of articles written after the popular author J. K. Rowling had an incident with cancel culture.

The debate is still wide open to interpretation.

> *"To preserve a free and open society, legal protections from government censorship, while crucial, are not nearly enough."*

Free Speech Is Necessary for Society to Evolve
Brad Polumbo

In the following viewpoint, Brad Polumbo argues that it is not only censorship by governments that is dangerous; self-censorship driven by culture is equally damaging. Free thought and discourse are cornerstones of a healthy, evolving society. When a culture inches toward self-censorship as a result of a population acting as "thought police," then fear and cowardice pervade. And with that, society remains stagnant because those in favor of the status quo remain silent and those who desire change are too afraid to speak out. Brad Polumbo is a libertarian-conservative journalist and opinion editor at the Foundation for Economic Education.

"Why George Orwell's Warning on 'Self-Censorship' Is More Relevant Than Ever," by Brad Polumbo, Foundation for Economic Education, July 17, 2020. https://fee.org/articles/why-george-orwells-warning-on-self-censorship-is-more-relevant-than-ever/. Licensed under CC BY 4.0 International.

As you read, consider the following questions:

1. Why does the author use George Orwell as a comparison to today's situation?
2. Why is protecting speech and thought beyond the law so important, according to the viewpoint?
3. Who described free speech as "the great moral renovator of society and government"?

Rule One: Speak your mind at your own peril. Rule Two: Never risk commissioning a story that goes against the narrative. Rule Three: Never believe an editor or publisher who urges you to go against the grain. Eventually, the publisher will cave to the mob, the editor will get fired or reassigned, and you'll be hung out to dry."

The above is a quotation from George Orwell's preface to *Animal Farm*, titled "The Freedom of the Press," where he discussed the chilling effect the Soviet Union's influence had on global publishing and debate far beyond the reach of its official censorship laws.

Wait, no it isn't. The quote is actually an excerpt from the resignation letter of *New York Times* opinion editor and writer Bari Weiss, penned this week, where she blows the whistle on the hostility toward intellectual diversity that now reigns supreme at the country's most prominent newspaper.

A contrarian moderate but hardly right-wing in her politics, the journalist describes the outright harassment and cruelty she faced at the hands of her colleagues, to the point where she could no longer continue her work:

> My own forays into Wrongthink have made me the subject of constant bullying by colleagues who disagree with my views. They have called me a Nazi and a racist; I have learned to brush off comments about how I'm "writing about the Jews again." Several colleagues perceived to be friendly with me were badgered by coworkers. My work and my character are openly demeaned on company-wide Slack channels where masthead

editors regularly weigh in. There, some coworkers insist I need to be rooted out if this company is to be a truly "inclusive" one, while others post ax emojis next to my name. Still other *New York Times* employees publicly smear me as a liar and a bigot on Twitter with no fear that harassing me will be met with appropriate action. They never are.

Weiss's letter reminds us of the crucial warning Orwell made in his time: To preserve a free and open society, legal protections from government censorship, while crucial, are not nearly enough.

To see why, simply consider the fate that has met Weiss and so many others in recent memory who dared cross the modern thought police. Here are just a few of the countless examples of "cancel culture" in action:

- A museum curator in San Francisco resigned after facing a mob and petition for his removal simply because he stated that his museum would still collect art from white men.
- A Palestinian immigrant and business owner had his lease canceled and restaurant boycotted after activists dug up his daughter's old offensive social media posts from when she was a teenager.
- A Hispanic construction worker was fired for making a supposedly "white supremacist" hand signal that for most people has always just meant "okay."
- A soccer player was pushed off the Los Angeles Galaxy roster because his wife posted something racist on Instagram.
- The head opinion editor of the *New York Times* was fired and his colleague was demoted after they published an op-ed by a US senator arguing a widely held position and liberal colleagues claimed the words "put black lives in danger."
- A random Boeing executive was recently mobbed and fired because he wrote an article 30 years ago arguing against having women serve in combat roles in the military.
- A data analyst tweeted out the findings of a research paper (by a black scholar) about the ineffectiveness of protests and was fired after colleagues claimed their safety was threatened.

- Led by progressives as prominent as *New York Times* columnist Paul Krugman, a woke mob tried to get a Chicago economist fired from his editorship of an economics journal for tweeting that embracing "Defund the Police" undercuts the Black Lives Matter movement's chances of achieving real reform.

These are just a few examples of many. One important commonality to note is that none of these examples involve actual government censorship. Yet they still represent chilling crackdowns on free speech. As David French put it writing for the *Dispatch*, "Cruelty bullies employers into firing employees. Cruelty bullies employees into leaving even when they're not fired. Cruelty raises the cost of speaking the truth as best you see it—until you find yourself choosing silence, mainly as a pain-avoidance mechanism."

These recent observations echo what Orwell warned of decades ago:

> Obviously it is not desirable that a government department should have any power of censorship... but the chief danger to freedom of thought and speech at this moment is not the direct interference of the [government] or any official body. If publishers and editors exert themselves to keep certain topics out of print, it is not because they are frightened of prosecution but because they are frightened of public opinion. In this country intellectual cowardice is the worst enemy a writer or journalist has to face, and that fact does not seem to me to have had the discussion it deserves.

Similarly, the British philosopher Bertrand Russell noted in a 1922 speech: "It is clear that thought is not free if the professional of certain opinions makes it impossible to earn a living."

Some might wonder why it's really so important to protect speech and thought beyond the law. After all, if no one's going to jail over it, how serious can the consequences really be?

While understandable as an impulse, this logic misses the point. Free and open speech is the only way a society can, through trial and error, get closer to the truth over time. It was abolitionist Frederick Douglass who described free speech as "the great moral renovator of society and government." What he meant was that only the free flow of open speech can challenge existing orthodoxies and evolve society. From women's suffrage to the civil rights movement, we never would have made so much progress on sexism and racism without the right to speak freely.

Silence enshrines the status quo. As John Stuart Mill put it:

> If the opinion is right, they are deprived of the opportunity of exchanging error for truth: if wrong, they lose, what is almost as great a benefit, the clearer perception and livelier impression of truth, produced by its collision with error.

This great discovery process through free-flowing speech first and foremost requires a hands-off approach from the government, but it still cannot occur in a culture hostile to dissenting opinion and debate. When airing a differing view can get you mobbed or put your job in jeopardy, only society's most powerful or those whose views align with the current orthodoxy will be able to speak openly without fear.

Orwell and Russell were right then, even if we're only fully realizing it now. Self-censorship driven by culture, not government, erodes our collective discovery of truth all the same.

> *"Cancel culture is one of the more complicated trends to hit the internet in recent years. Some argue that it's too harsh, others argue that it just doesn't have any real consequences."*

Everyone Is Getting Canceled

Logan Mahan

In the following viewpoint, Logan Mahan argues that cancel culture is a nuanced and often puzzling trend with many gray areas. While call-out culture has been especially helpful for communities with less power, the mob mentality of cancel culture can be extremely toxic. The author calls for educating people instead of canceling them, so they—and we—can learn from their mistakes. Logan Mahan is the assistant editor of Insidehook.com and has written for the Houston Chronicle, *the* Seattle Post-Intelligencer, Her Campus, Greenwich Time, Stamford Advocate, RealClearLife, and RootsRated, *among other publications.*

"Youthsplaining: Everything You Need to Know About Cancel Culture," by Logan Mahan, Inside Hook (insidehook.com), August 20, 2019. Reprinted by permission.

As you read, consider the following questions:

1. How did Taylor Swift describe her experience with cancel culture?
2. Is cancel culture good or bad, according to the author?
3. How does being canceled affect—or not affect—a person's fanbase?

The cancellations never stop pouring in—and I'm not talking about all the shows Netflix has decided to end so abruptly. I'm talking about all the times we "cancel" celebrities, media personalities and really anyone with a social media platform we decide they're using inappropriately.

You may have heard the term "cancel culture" pop up just last week when comedian Sarah Silverman said on an episode of "The Bill Simmons Podcast" that she thought "cancel culture" should itself be canceled, adding that social shaming is "really scary" and referring to the whole thing as "righteousness porn." Silverman was fired from a movie recently, after a 2007 photo of her in blackface resurfaced, even though she has since apologized for the photo, going so far as to draw attention to it in an interview for *GQ* last year. The comedian argued on the podcast that cancel culture leaves no room for growth.

"I'm not saying, 'Don't hold me accountable,'" she said. "I held myself accountable. I can't erase that I did that, but I can only be changed forever and do what I can to make it right for the rest of my life."

When two allegations of sexual misconduct against Katy Perry were reported last week, there was a small campaign on Twitter to cancel the singer—evidence of which you can find when you search the hashtags #KatyPerryIsOverParty (the customizable hashtag format typically used in cancelation campaigns) or #SurvivingKatyPerry, a play on the "Surviving R. Kelly" documentary that exposed his history of sexual assault.

However, those tweets are few in comparison to other historic cancelations, which is probably because we don't take sexual misconduct allegations against women as seriously as we do those against men, which, yes I know, is f**ked up. It can also be because Perry has a swarm of dedicated fans, hell bent on convincing the world of her innocence, who created the counter hashtag #KatyPerryIsLovedParty.

Cancel culture is one of the more complicated trends to hit the internet in recent years. Some argue that it's too harsh, others argue that it just doesn't have any real consequences. Certainly it has ruined people's reputations and chances at business opportunities, in many cases rightly so, but it has also created a mob-like mentality thereby any minuscule mistake makes it open season for intense backlash.

But there's a lot to unpack here so we might as well get to it.

Ok, So What Exactly Is Cancel Culture?

According to Wikipedia—yes, there is a Wikipedia page—there are two variant terms for the trend. The term call-out culture is a form of public shaming which occurs on social media (usually Twitter) that aims to hold people accountable by calling attention to behavior that is deemed problematic. Cancel culture is a form of boycott in which someone, typically a celeb, has shared a questionable opinion, or again, has had problematic behavior called out on social media. That person is then "canceled," which essentially means they're boycotted by a large number of people, sometimes leading to massive declines in the person's fanbase and career.

This usually begins when a person says or expresses an opinion that is racist/sexist/homophobic/transphobic/xenophobic. Most often it is something that person has said in their distant past that has been found and re-posted, bringing new attention to it. This can be screenshots of old tweets or old videos that resurface of the problematic behavior in question.

These types of cancellations have been especially prominent in the world of beauty YouTubers. In 2018, make-up artist Laura Lee lost over 300,000 subscribers on her YouTube channel and had businesses and sponsors sever ties with her after tweets from 2012 resurfaced that showed her making racist remarks. She uploaded a 4-minute apology video that was criticized for being insincere and for her apparent "fake crying," which then eventually became a meme.

But it can happen for bigger name celebrities too. Kevin Hart stepped down from hosting the 2019 Oscars because of resurfaced homophobic tweets, with much of Twitter, including celebs, calling out his behavior. This eventually got the attention of the Academy who asked Hart to apologize. The backlash only increased after Hart refused to apologize, and it was only after he announced he was stepping down from hosting duties that an apology also ensued.

Then there are the cancelations that can occur from less severe circumstances. Back in 2016, Taylor Swift was "canceled" after the internet accused her of "always playing the victim" after she got into a feud with Kim Kardashian and Kanye West over a lyric in West's song "Famous." Kim K called Swift a snake, using the snake emoji, of course, and pretty much the entire rest of the internet followed suit.

In a recent interview with *Vogue*, Swift said that the entire experience felt isolating. "I don't think there are that many people who can actually understand what it's like to have millions of people hate you very loudly," said Swift. "When you say someone is canceled, it's not a TV show. It's a human being. You're sending mass amounts of messaging to this person to either shut up, disappear, or it could also be perceived as, Kill yourself."

So Is Cancel Culture Good or Bad?

Well, it's complicated. Calling out someone, especially someone who has great influence, for their harmful behavior or ideas is something that we should continue to do. Call-out culture has especially been helpful for people of color and LGBTQIA+ communities in keeping their spaces free of s**tty people.

But then many have also brought up that the mob-mentality of cancel culture can be toxic, and as Sarah Silverman pointed out, these mass social media campaigns against a person can actually hinder them from growing and learning from their mistakes. Instead of "canceling" them, we should be educating them.

Fine, But Is "Canceling" Someone Actually Effective?

It depends, and it's not necessarily even clear on what.

Another beauty guru, Jeffree Star, was also called out during the time of Laura Lee's cancellation for saying the N-word in an old video. But while Lee was pretty much canceled for good, Star is still one of the most popular people on YouTube, with over 15 million subscribers, a wildly successful makeup brand and millions of followers across other social media platforms.

Taylor Swift has gone through the wringer of "cancelations" as well, and she's still the #1 female artist in the world. Kanye West was "canceled" for his support of Trump, Kim Kardashian gets called out almost daily for culture appropriation—yet they've still got millions of fans and will remain among the richest people in the world.

Many have argued that cancel culture exists only in the Twitter bubble. It can seem as if a celeb's entire existence is finished when thousands of users start hashtagging "___IsOverParty," but in the real world, it might not even cross people's minds. Which might be why bigger name celebs have an easier time bouncing back from scandals, and why YouTubers and Instagram influencers whose businesses and brands live solely in the realm of the internet are more often the subjects of cancelation campaigns—and have a harder time bouncing back.

Plus having a large army of diehard fans willing to clutter feeds with tweets in your defense, like in the case of Katy Perry, can also help higher-powered celebs come back from the cancelation dead.

Does Cancel Culture Even Exist?

I'm not even quite sure what "cancel culture" is, or even if it has been clearly defined. Where do you draw the line between a society threatening "cancel culture" and robust disagreements that might have gone further than we might like? How do we distinguish between someone justifiably objecting to what another person is promoting, and them trying to unacceptably silence/cancel the other person? When is it okay for an organisation to penalise one of their members for what they've said publicly and when should we expect organisations to defend their members in the interests of free speech, even if they also object to what was said?

My issue with this narrative is partly based on my experiences in the public climate debate. Most of those who complain about censorship, or being silenced/cancelled, seem to be those who say things that deserve to be criticised and simply don't want to engage with their critics; it's more about deligitimising one's critics, than defending free speech.

This, of course, doesn't mean that one shouldn't be concerned about attacks on free speech. It doesn't mean that some of what is highlighted in the context "cancel culture" aren't things that decent people should object to. However, we should also be careful of dealing with things like this in ways that end up deligitimising valid criticisms, and undermining valid social movements. In fact, I can't quite see how we can deal with some kind of "cancel culture" (however defined) that doesn't end up doing the very thing we're trying to avoid.

"Cancel Culture?" … and Then There's Physics, July 9, 2020.

What's certain is that cancel culture has started to lose its impact in recent years. Maybe because at times it has spiraled out of control and been used for the wrong reasons, forcing people to start questioning it. Or maybe we've become immune since people in high places—the highest of all the places, one might say—can now say and do whatever they want without being held accountable or subject to any consequences. As but a youth, who am I to say?

> *"Civil discourse demands that democratic participants respect each other, even when that respect is hard to give or to earn. Democratic societies must be societies where arguments are tolerated and encouraged, but this is not always easy."*

Learning to Engage in Civil Discourse Could Prevent Canceling

Kate Shuster

In the following viewpoint, Kate Shuster argues that there is a way to debate divisive issues in a productive and respectful way. This entails being civil, which is not the same as being polite. Civil discourse supports, rather than undermines, the societal good. The author notes that students can be given the tools for civil discourse through school curricula. Kate Shuster is a researcher and author based in Montgomery, Alabama. She also manages the Teaching Hard History project, where she promotes debate education, produces podcasts and films, and evaluates teaching initiatives.

"Toward a More Civil Discourse," by Kate Shuster, Southern Poverty Law Center, *Teaching Tolerance*, Issue 37, Spring 2010. Reprinted with the permission of Teaching Tolerance, a project of the Southern Poverty Law Center. www.tolerance.org.

As you read, consider the following questions:

1. What does the author mean by "a more civil discourse"?
2. How does the 24/7 news cycle contribute to discord in public debate?
3. What is the origin of the word "civility," according to the viewpoint?

There is a pressing need to change the tenor of public debate from shouts and slurs to something more reasoned and effective. But it is difficult for teachers already burdened with standardized tests and administrative duties to find the time to craft lessons to teach civil discourse in their classrooms. To support teachers working to change the terms of our national debate, Teaching Tolerance offers a new curriculum entitled "Civil Discourse in the Classroom and Beyond."

We live in a climate ripe with noise: Media outlets and 24-hour news cycles mean that everyone with access to a computer has access to a megaphone to broadcast their views. Never before in human history has an opinion had the opportunity to reach so many so quickly without regard to its accuracy or appropriateness.

It is difficult to hear anything when everyone has a megaphone. For young people trying to learn how to speak and listen, this is an especially complicated business.

"The lesson learned is a dangerous one," says Danielle Wiese Leek, assistant professor in the School of Communications at Grand Valley State University in Allendale, Mich. "First, it's anti-democratic. It's not about learning to be exposed to a variety of perspectives in order to draw the best conclusion. It teaches young people that if they aren't the loudest, their opinion doesn't matter. Second, it shuts down opportunities for collaboration and innovation. Some of the best ideas that have been produced throughout human history came from people working together."

TOLERANCE FROM A GLOBAL PERSPECTIVE

In an age where the electronic media has drawn us closer together into what is called a global village, or a global society, its benefits will only be felt when mutual goodness prevails, when mutual respect and understanding prevail.

If, instead of good feelings, hatred emerges, if restlessness usurps heartfelt peace, then we **must** accept that this is not progress, but is something that will take us towards unexpected results.

In this globalisation, where people of different backgrounds, cultures and religions are living together, and where the world has become multicultural and full of diversity, establishing tolerance and harmony has become very crucial and important, and fostering mutual love and affection has become vital.

Without tolerance and harmony the lasting peace of societies cannot be maintained, and loyalty for each other cannot be established.

Loyalty is borne from feelings of love and affection. At a personal level the feelings of love strengthens the feelings of loyalty. When a citizen loves his country, he exhibits loyalty and devotion and makes sacrifices for the sake of the nation.

If sentiments of love do not exist, then the spirit of sacrifice cannot be formed. Unless a person loves another he can never have good feelings in his heart towards him, and he cannot faithfully fulfil the rights due to that person.

Lack of tolerance leads to fighting, violence, and finally it destroys the peace and security of society. When people fail in their arguments they become intolerant, and then they use force and aggression to support their point of view.

We have seen considerable incidents in recent history where, because of lack of tolerance, people have attacked people of other faiths, their places of worship, their communities. How nice it would be if everyone tried to express himself in a decent and respectful way with tolerance.

The world is full of diversity, and that is the beauty of our universe. If there had not been any diversity, the world would appear boring and unattractive, and without any competition.

"Importance of Tolerance," by Laiq Ahmed Atif, *Times of Malta*, December 26, 2010.

Educators are well positioned to provide a counterweight to this loudest-is-best approach. Schools and classrooms strive to be safe places where students can exchange ideas, try out opinions and receive feedback on their ideas without fear or intimidation.

Children, of course, often come to school with opinions or prejudices they have learned in their homes or from the media. Schools can become a place of intolerance and fear, especially for students who voice minority opinions.

Schools, then, must work to be the site of social transformation, where teachers and young people find ways to communicate effectively.

This is not simply about being polite.

As University of North Carolina Chapel Hill Assistant Professor of Rhetoric Chris Lundberg says, "There are times when a certain degree of impoliteness is called for. If we say we are only going to allow polite discourse in the public sphere, we are writing off the first group of women who wanted political suffrage, because at the time that was seen as impolite."

The key word, then, is civility.

"The idea of civility … originates in Cicero with the concept of the *societas civilus*," Lundberg explains. "What it meant was that there are certain standards of conduct towards others and that members of the civil society should comport themselves in a way that sought the good of the city. The old concept of civility was much more explicitly political than our current notion of politeness. Speech was filtered through how it did or did not contribute to the good of the city."

Civil discourse is discourse that supports, rather than undermines, the societal good. It demands that democratic participants respect each other, even when that respect is hard to give or to earn. Democratic societies must be societies where arguments are tolerated and encouraged, but this is not always easy.

"To engage in a healthy political argument is to acknowledge the possibility that one's own arguments could be falsified or proven wrong," says Thomas Hollihan, professor at the University of Southern California's Annenberg School of Communication. "This demands that citizens listen respectfully to the claims made by others. Name-calling, threats and bullying behaviors do not meet the demands of effective deliberation."

This new curriculum—based on lessons tested in diverse classrooms across the United States and proven effective with a wide range of students and topics—will introduce educators to basic tools for teaching civil discourse. It is not subject-specific; on the contrary, the tools of argumentation and discussion lend themselves to any subject in any classroom. Although it is primarily designed for young adolescents, the curriculum can be adapted for students of any age.

Using these lessons, students will be able to turn their unsubstantiated opinions into reasoned arguments. They also will learn how to effectively challenge an opposing argument—not with fists and fury, but rather with a step-by-step process for refutation.

These tools lay the groundwork for productive, reasoned and lively discussions on a variety of topics. They also will give students "training wheels" for learning how to have reasoned arguments outside the classroom.

> *"Continually canceling old figures as we update our definition of 'woke' or 'PC' will lead to the obliteration of our most important works as a species. There would be no historical mistakes to learn from, nor successes to admire."*

Cancel Culture Is Jeopardizing the Education of Young People

Thomas Ullman

In the following viewpoint, Thomas Ullman argues that the current environment of cancel culture is rampant in schools and is damaging to young people. The author points out that boycotting books that include language that is no longer acceptable in today's society, such as Mark Twain's The Adventures of Huckleberry Finn, *deprives students of those works. More troubling, it removes the opportunity for students to learn from the mistakes of the past. And that could doom them to repeating those mistakes in the future. Thomas Ullman is a high school student attending Marin Academy in California.*

As you read, consider the following questions:

1. Why have some schools canceled *The Adventures of Huckleberry Finn*?
2. Why is Aristotle suddenly controversial?
3. What does the author mean when he calls the current culture "Orwellian"?

In my tenth grade English class, just like many other American students, I read some of the works of the late Joseph Conrad, an unbounded explorer and captivating writer.

But my class did not analyze Conrad's books as my father or grandfather did when they were my age.

Instead of discussing how his works shaped authors-to-come and how his novels were some of the earliest modernist ones, we debated whether or not he should even be taught in the classroom.

We did not study the stories of exploration and tragedy that captivated the many authors who shaped the Western psyche; rather, we had long arguments over whether or not to cast him out of the literary canon entirely because of some of his racially insensitive statements, which in his time were not unorthodox.

Put simply, we were taught to throw the baby out with the bathwater—to hold past figures like Conrad to a modern standard unthinkable for those of his era, and to throw those who could not meet such standards out of the libraries of our schools.

One year later, I have grown to see cancel culture intensify with the capricious nature of political debate in 2020, with some of humanity's most pivotal philosophers and writers like Aristotle and Shakespeare being its current targets. While the immediate consequences may be hard to see, our youth—the future of our nation—will ultimately end up having to pay the price for America's cancel culture.

Some of the country's schools, pushed by activists and influencers to embrace cancel culture, have begun focusing on the supposed harm of individual out-of-context words without understanding their broader meaning in a text.

For example, in 2019, members of the New Jersey state government attempted to remove Mark Twain's *The Adventures of Huckleberry Finn* from the state's educational institutions, citing numerous uses of racial slurs and stereotypes. But the 19th century book, which shares the title of "Great American Novel" with the likes of *The Great Gatsby* and *To Kill a Mockingbird*, is in fact an anti-racist one. It unmasks the racist falsehoods that were used to justify slavery for centuries, while also showcasing the humanity of enslaved characters and bringing an egalitarian message to readers.

Unfortunately, the near-sighted crowd that wants to ban this book from schools has failed to critically analyze the book's meaning. The usage of the n-word in the novel to showcase racist attitudes moved many to press for its removal from America's literary canon. Some schools have already heeded their words.

The idea is that the removal of such a novel will shield the nation's schoolchildren from bigoted words and sentiments, but this will not be the real outcome.

By removing *The Adventures of Huckleberry Finn* from our schools, we lose one of the most influential anti-racist books of our time.

Continually canceling old figures as we update our definition of "woke" or "PC" will lead to the obliteration of our most important works as a species. There would be no historical mistakes to learn from, nor successes to admire.

We would be left on an artificial and isolated loop of history—and if we cannot teach the nation's youth about the problems of the past, they are bound to imitate them in the future.

Mark Twain's novel was obviously one that spoke out against racism, but what about figures who outright supported bigoted views? Are they to be tossed into the dustbin of history?

Aristotle, who is regarded as one of the greatest philosophers to ever live, was himself openly supportive of slavery. Only several weeks ago, the *New York Times* published a piece that argued against the cancellation of Aristotle for these views. It was met with criticism from professors such as Bryan W. Van Norden, who stated that "[professors] also need to remember that among our students are people who have felt firsthand the continuing practical consequences of Aristotle's more heinous views."

Now, of course, nobody (and especially not me) is arguing that we should be defending Aristotle's views against equality, which belong in antiquity. But it is important to remember his positive contributions to modern political theory, physics, economics, and psychology—some things that we, in the modern era, regard as integral parts of Western civilization.

Should we cast away the remainder of Aristotle's thoughts and ideas because of a few bad apples? We would lose some of the very foundations of the modern world.

In addition, it is unreasonable to hold the "heinous" beliefs of ancient figures to modern ethical standards. Instead of ignoring their thoughts as a whole, we should understand their faults and teach them to our youth, so they understand why our society deems them to be unacceptable.

All that being said, Professor Van Norden's statement resonated at first with me. As a Jewish person myself, I have cringed at works like William Shakespeare's *The Merchant of Venice*, which contains highly stereotypical depictions of Jewish people. Many of these stereotpyes ended up influencing centuries of antisemitic sentiment in Europe and worldwide.

Nevertheless, I have come to understand that the Bard's other works—*Macbeth*, *Romeo and Juliet*, and *Hamlet*—have all had profound positive impacts on literature. Rest assured, I won't be trying to cancel Shakespeare anytime soon.

The burden of a society that continually condemns old figures as progressive quotas change with time lies on the students of America. It is nothing short of Orwellian: yesterday, at war with Eurasia, tomorrow, at war with Eastasia. Yesterday, reading Aristotle, tomorrow, burning his works in the name of progressivism.

I introduced my experiences with Joseph Conrad's books in the beginning of this article for a very important reason: the alternative introduction to his novels that my class was given was not just a simple trigger warning. It foreshadowed a long, dark path of literary suppression, one that will continue to significantly limit intellectual domains in the pursuit of a society free of offense at the cost of our most beloved texts: a society where ignorance is strength.

> *"We live in a world where the simple and dichotomous statements of one two-syllable word can doom a brand. But unlike a boycott, the word* canceled *bars any chance for redemption."*

Social Media's "Cancel Culture" Calls Out the Wrong Brands

Alain Sylvain

In the following viewpoint, Alain Sylvain argues that cancel culture can sometimes go horribly wrong. The author calls out brands that may have been perceived as doing something immoral, often due to the influencers they work with. But lost in the triumph of "woke" call-out culture is the notion that perfectly fine individuals and brands can become casualties due to one misstep. And recovery can be disproportionately challenging. Alain Sylvain is the founder and CEO of Sylvain Labs, an innovation and brand design consultancy company with offices in New York City, Amsterdam, and Richmond, Virginia.

"Social Media's 'Cancel Culture' Calls Out the Wrong Brands," by Alain Sylvain, Quartz Media, August 1, 2019. Reprinted by permission.

As you read, consider the following questions:

1. What industry does the author note is rampant with cancel culture?
2. What does the author say about actually canceling cancel culture?
3. What role do influencers play in cancel culture cases?

In 2015, Chichi Eburu spotted a gap in the beauty market: There was nothing that represented black culture as a whole.

Sure, there were a growing number of brands offering more than 40 shades of foundation, but there wasn't an alternative that was unapologetically and authentically tied to the beauty needs and culture of black women.

So with $2,000, the stay-at-home mom started a beauty brand out of her two-bedroom apartment and named it Juvia's Place, after her two children. Eburu started building capital by selling makeup brushes and tools and funneled it into a palette called the Nubian. Comprised of deep bronzes and golds, she used Queen Nefertiti's likeness to brand the palette, cementing Juvia's Place as a makeup brand for black women, by black women. The product not only changed Eburu's life, but according to one beauty blogger, "the way in which we view black women in the beauty industry today."

As Eburu hit the beauty trade-show circuit in 2016, the Nubian palette went viral on Instagram after several glowing reviews, and carved out a permanent place for her in the industry.

So when the brand ventured into foundation last month, once-upon-a-time Myspace musician turned beauty vlogger and influencer Jeffree Star made sure he was amongst the first to check out the new product. He rushed to mega beauty store Ulta to pick up several shades before trying them out on camera. He was "thoroughly impressed," according to his review. "For an indie brand to come on the market with their first-ever foundation, they're killing it, let's just say that right now," he said.

With more than 15 million YouTube followers, the words "Jeffree Star approved" can make or break a product. So naturally, Juvia's Place posted about the review on their Instagram, thanking the influencer for his support:

> We're speechless. Shade Cairo in I Am Magic foundation. Jeffree found his match in @ultabeauty. Did you find your match? Comment below. Thank you @jeffreestar.

Almost instantly, the brand was hit with brutal backlash online. "Is it a trend among black businesses to say F**K BLACK CONSUMERS upon reaching a certain level of fame even tho those same consumers were there from day UNO?" one critic commented.

And just like that, Juvia's Place was "canceled."

The brand was rejected not just by consumers, but by the same black beauty influencers who helped Juvia's Place achieve its level of success. Many now refuse to support the brand in any way, shape or form.

And even though Juvia's Place has since deleted that post, the damage has been done.

The New Boycott

Cancel culture, also and perhaps more formally known as call-out culture, is the boycott of the social media economy. It occurs when social media users publicly call out brands and celebrities from missteps.

According to Urban Dictionary, "In pop culture, canceled means to make someone or something irrelevant due to current drama."

It's also defined as "to dismiss something or somebody. To reject an individual or an idea."

Think of it as a boycott for the attention economy. Rather than refusing to buy a product or service from a brand that has views that differ from our own, we refuse to pay attention to a brand (or person, an influencer) that has views different from our own. We stop following them, reducing their follower count, and therefore their value in our social media-driven economy.

Sometimes, this is a useful way to ensure social accountability, as when celebrities and executives have been outed for abusive behavior. But mob-mentality social media campaigns also risk sweeping undeserving brands along in a controversy, and overlooking important complexities in the process.

The "Drama"

So what exactly happened? Despite having amassed a massive social following and being the fifth-highest paid YouTuber, Star has a well-documented history of making racist comments. And, for a brand that proudly positions itself as part of the "for us, by us" culture, celebrating the beauty vlogger's influence felt like a betrayal for many—and inauthentic at the very least.

Rather than propelling a fledgling start-up to the mainstream, Star's review—or more specifically, Juvia's Place's celebration of his review—was enough to effectively cancel the brand.

The irony is deafening. After videos of Star making racist comments hit the mainstream, he issued a heartfelt apology that seemingly absolved him, or at least protected his follower account, and removed him from the brink of cancelation.

In the video, he acknowledged the weight that being a social media influencer held. And the controversy seemed to die down.

The case of Star illustrates that there is a good social function to the act of canceling—just like there traditionally is for socially conscious boycotting. By reducing the cultural cache of those in power, it forces them to change behavior that we deem socially unacceptable. It's how we assert our power, and it can be used as a force for good.

Not All Canceling Is Created Equal

Juvia's Place is a black-owned brand, which was canceled by black influencers because of a controversial endorsement. But what does it say about our society that we're so quick to cancel Juvia's Place, yet so forgiving of someone like Star and the global brands that make potentially harmful public mistakes on a massive scale—think Pepsi, H&M, Nike, Dove, Uber?

It's a complicated web of accountability and resources, as it turns out.

By canceling Juvia's Place, consumers stripped it of its cultural relevance, and power. In many cases, established or legacy brands survive in this cultural minefield, while small brands struggle, because large brands can still buy our attention spans, while small brands rely on word-of-mouth and influencer marketing. Smaller brands, and especially smaller minority-led brands, simply don't have the reputation or resources to course-correct, further empowering the untethered reach of the corporations that do.

Peak Culture?

Looking at how we use the word *cancel* gives us insight into how we've reached this tipping point. Cancel culture is particularly rampant in the beauty industry. James Charles, the first male face of CoverGirl, was absolutely obliterated after feuding with another beauty YouTuber, losing more than 3 million followers on Instagram over the course of a few days. Kim Kardashian was almost canceled after initially naming her shapewear line "Kimono," which social media users deemed culturally insensitive.

Cancel culture is so rampant in the beauty industry because the market is so defined by influencers. Beauty influencers market themselves as personalities, and are therefore judged and consumed as personalities. If consumers dislike features of a product, they usually dismiss it. If fans dislike the ethos of an influencer, they do the same.

But as influencers become more and more, well, influential in other industries, and we become more and more used to interacting with brands, products, and services on social platforms, cancel culture is growing. And potentially, we've reached peak.

Yara Shahidi—canceled. Shania Twain—canceled for vocally supporting Trump. Kanye West—canceled for reasons he explains himself: "I'm canceled. I'm canceled because I didn't cancel Trump."

And most recently, in perhaps the most 2019 moment of the year so far, the Dalai Lama was canceled following sexist remarks.

Influence Imbalances

Brands and celebrities used to wield so much power, it bordered on arrogance. A brand could espouse its belief on people with little fear of ramifications. Think about all the examples of advertising from the 80s, with exclusionary messages of Americana and the good life at the forefront.

My, how the tables have turned. Now consumers risk acting with the same sense of arrogance. With the help of influencers, they wield incredible power over a brand's reputation, in the form of online commentators waiting on the sidelines for someone to make a wrong play. This comes with a justification that online commentators determine what's right and what's wrong.

It's getting dangerous. We live in a world where the simple and dichotomous statements of one two-syllable word can doom a brand. But unlike a boycott, the word *canceled* bars any chance for redemption.

With cancel culture, we're facing the tyranny of the masses. Much like French historian Alexis de Tocqueville concluded, perhaps we need a balance of power to check ourselves. In a social-media-driven world, if consumers wield the power and influencers have become our new representatives, do brands need to act as the judicial branch?

Brands could hold influencers to higher standards, much like the judicial branch holds the executive and legislative branch to constitutional standards in the government. If influencers represent the masses, they are political representatives and need to be held to the same level of scrutiny that we hold our candidates. There should be rules of engagement, influencer watch-dogs, and audits of influence and importance.

Cancel culture will only become less brutal if we change the way we react to it. Let's stop looking at things along such dichotomous lines and stop being so afraid to make missteps. We need to own when we get something wrong, and start asserting our power and our social responsibility on others that do, too. But most importantly, we need to be more constructive about it.

Can We Cancel Culture? (No.)

The point is, cancel culture can't be canceled. You can't take away someone's right to assert their opinion, even if the way in which it has manifested is toxic. Large brands and celebrities should lead the way in changing the narrative around cancel culture, and restore its original intent.

A colleague of mine asked what I would do if I was the founder of Juvia's Place. After reflecting on it for a while, I realized it would be a moment to assert my own values, without calling out someone else's: "Thank you for recognizing us. We know you have great influence and your endorsement is powerful. But we would be remiss if we didn't call attention to this and the furor of many of our own followers. We take our role seriously and believe this is an opportunity to channel our user."

But we all know hindsight is 20/20. The reason cancel culture continues to rule brands, and the reason it is so powerful, is that it often preys on the unintended consequences of an action or a remark. Perhaps brands can lead here by imparting the PR-minded strategies of considering all the consequences for a remark, and reposition their power as leaders in the public sphere.

> *"Cancel culture can prove damaging*
> *to the social status of the enemies*
> *of a group or a person and this*
> *is empowering to those doing the*
> *'canceling' because of the benefits*
> *that can, at times, be derived."*

Participating in Cancel Culture Increases a Person's Social Status

Michael Toebe

In the following viewpoint, Michael Toebe argues that there may be a psychological reason for the popularity of cancel culture. The author notes that the act of taking someone down can help move a person up the social ladder. In addition, expressing moral outrage can garner trust from others. However, the author cautions that we all should be aware of disproportionate or cruel reactions. Michael Toebe is a specialist on reputation, professional communication, and wise crisis management. He writes a weekly newsletter on Medium.

"What Drives Social Media Mobbing?" by Michael Toebe, Corporate Compliance Insights, January 9, 2020. Reprinted by permission.

As you read, consider the following questions:

1. Why is calling out bad behavior risky?

2. What are some solutions the author emphasizes as an answer to cancel culture?

3. What makes the internet so prone to incidents of cancel culture?

Social media is a powerful voice in society, whether led by media, people of high influence in different professions or in the court of public opinion. All can be provoked emotionally when it comes to other people's transgressions or perceived violations of social expectations.

There is a term for the judgment and punishment that regularly develops from this aggressive, punitive echo chamber: social mobbing.

Why Is Social Mobbing So Attractive?

An excellent article detailing this social psychology and behavior was published recently in *Psychology Today*. "5 Reasons Why People Love Cancel Culture—Research Reveals Why Social Media Mobs Enjoy Cancelling People," written by Rob Henderson, reveals important, valuable research findings.

Henderson, a Gates Cambridge Scholar and Ph.D. student at the University of Cambridge, is a veteran of the US Air Force and did his undergraduate work at Yale University (B.S., Psychology) upon leaving the service.

The catalyst for his article on the cancel culture was rooted in meaningful observation and the curiosity it stimulated.

"Four days after being honorably discharged from the military, I matriculated to Yale as an undergraduate. Within two months, I observed as students targeted a lecturer because she defended freedom of expression. They successfully pushed her out of her position as a faculty member," Henderson said. That type of cultural aggression repeated itself in his next surroundings.

"Four months after matriculating to Cambridge as a graduate student, I observed students target a professor. They successfully revoked his invitation to join Cambridge as a guest research fellow. This has been my introduction to higher education in the US and the UK," he said.

The research findings are valuable to organizational leaders because they clearly detail the psychological drivers (motivation) that make social mobbing attractive for those who participate.

To know is to understand, and with that understanding can come improved risk management and, when necessary, higher-quality problem solving through adversity or crisis with the media, social media and court of public opinion.

Research has found that participating in cancel culture can and does increase a person's social status, creating new opportunities to move up that figurative ladder by taking others down, which can prove a strong psychological motivation for some people. Does it prove effective?

"Research has indeed shown that expressing moral outrage can make others trust you more. It can serve as a signal of trustworthiness," Henderson said. "The logic is that if I see you target someone for alleged misconduct, then I will infer that you are a good person."

There are risks in this behavior though, he said.

"Still, other research shows that this can backfire," Henderson said. "If I learn you are a hypocrite—for example, that you target others for behavior you yourself engage in—then I will subsequently be less likely to trust you."

Cancel culture can prove damaging to the social status of the enemies of a group or a person and this is empowering to those doing the "canceling" because of the benefits that can, at times, be derived. Henderson shares how that can work in theory and practice.

He wrote that "one person losing social rank is the same as (the aggressor) gaining it. The research shows people engage in moral grandstanding to enhance their social rank. If you're a 'six' on the social-status ladder, working up to a 'nine' is hard. But scheming to bring a 'nine' down to a 'three' is easier and more thrilling."

That reward can be enticing to emotionally triggered people or those flooded in emotion. "If you see someone do something wrong and you feel a sense of righteous indignation, that might be a good time to think carefully about how to proceed, especially if others have already scolded the individual," Henderson said.

"Pointing out wrongdoing can be good for society," he said. "But most of us believe in proportional punishment. If I share or post something that is hurtful, it might be reasonable for you to point it out. But when 1,000 people 'like' your admonishment, and 1,000 more pile on with more vicious comments, then perhaps we've lost that sense of proportionality in the digital age."

It seems wise for protection for the benefit of our safety and well-being to consider our decisions and actions, because how we are perceived—our reputation—is not always in alignment with how the world can and will judge us. It is critical to consider the lay of the land, the culture, as organizations and individuals.

As to why a segment of society has come to believe their role is as legitimate, ultimate judge of people's well-being and arbiter of who is to be protected and who isn't… it's an interesting tribal question for a developed nation.

"This is a big question. One with several plausible answers. One answer is that all of us, to some extent, enjoy seeing our foes suffer. In the age of social media, some individuals have managed to use it as a tool to inflict pain on their adversaries," Henderson said. "You may have observed that social mobs choose their targets not based on whether they have done something wrong, but based on the faction to which they belong."

Again, back to impressions, judgments and reputation. This is valuable insight to have to conduct the wisest, strongest, risk management.

What targets of cancel culture might not always consider or remember is the connective value that social media mobbing provides. It's a sense of belonging, maybe sharing similarities to that of a gang.

Is there a healthy replacement for the behavior of mobbing, that dark satisfaction of aggression and schadenfreude?

"There are other ways to strengthen social bonds and unite around a common purpose. Helping others is deeply rewarding and need not come at the cost of singling out a perpetrator," Henderson said. "Affirming the values of one's group by helping them succeed can be just as rewarding, if not more so, as denigrating the behavior of others."

Does this create a sense of emotionally rewarding justice in mobs? Does it restore hope or some balance to life, soothe some pain or discontent?

"It's possible that cancel culture has flourished because it facilitates symbolic victories. Many problems in society run far deeper than any one person, but making an example of someone can make social mobs feel as if they are making a difference in the world," he said.

That is something for individuals or organizations to remember and plan to avoid: being in a position because of their beliefs, attitudes, impulses and behavior, where they can be judged and mobbed. Social media also provides easy thinking for mobs.

"We also like simple stories," Henderson said. "When deep problems get solved, they are often told in the form of data and statistics. Boring. When a person gets canceled, it arouses a sense of primitive triumph. Exciting."

What hope is there for psychology as a field to learn of better solutions to help society find a remedy for this type of impulse and behavior?

"Psychology has done a good job revealing how people can derive pleasure from unsavory acts," Henderson said. "Sharing such results can perhaps curb destructive patterns. Lack of awareness about our evolved impulses makes us more likely to enact them."

What Henderson has learned and communicated in his work is of critical importance for executives and boards of directors to understand. The findings are knowledge that can aid in decision analysis and decision-making in regards to governance, compliance, communications and, when relevant, crisis communications.

Preventative measures can mitigate the likelihood of social media mobbing and allow organizations to navigate through it with less risk and damages.

What Preventive Measures Will Prove Successful?

Consider the impact of decision-making and organizational actions. Do they align with cultural expectations of ethics and morality? Do they take into account how you want to be viewed for your interactions with your people, market and society? Do they reveal your best self while in pursuit of objectives?

Don't answer these questions alone. Invite feedback and encourage dissenting views. Create psychological safety to facilitate this critical information gathering. Seek what you might be missing. This approach can prove highly protective and act as improved risk management, governance and thus, quality "insurance" against social media attacks and the accompanying hunger for mobbing for a common purpose and engaging in cancel culture.

Regularly invest time in gaining a strong understanding of and practicing emotional intelligence principles. While this may seem abstract, impractical and of little value, on the contrary, it can prove invaluable as a reputation builder and next-level quality of risk management. Not surprisingly, the benefits will materialize within the organization as much as outside of it, creating increased benefit of the doubt in both places.

Set in place an early-response system to conflict that could end up in the media and social media or already has done so. Engage,

Social Media and Public Shaming

Social media is a dehumanization machine—which is ironic, given that it's also a great connector. You can ruin someone's day from across the planet. And you can do it without the guilt or anxiety of a face-to-face confrontation, because social media reduces people to a handle, a profile, or just an opinion.

Even the etymology of public shaming is inherently dehumanizing. In 2019, we talk of people being "cancelled," as though they're unpopular TV shows, and not human beings. And I suppose "cancelled" sounds more palatable than "ruined," "abused," or "driven to emotional and mental despair."

Worst of all, social media feeds into our primal desire for vengeance. It facilitates the kind of mob rule that predates our current system of jurisprudence, and was typified by people crouched locked in stocks, or branded with hot irons. Right-minded people should be absolutely terrified by this regression.

The Internet is brutal at the best of times, but add in a bit of righteous anger, and it gets worse. [Simone] Burns, a privileged white woman [publicly shamed for] racially abusing an Indian attendant, made a tantalizing target. It's reasonable to think that the stress from being a figure of hate overwhelmed her, driving Burns to take her own life.

People's lives are being ruined—and yes, sometimes ended—without the framework and proportionality of ordinary jurisprudence. Sometimes it's over actual crimes; while other times it's about crimes against the prevailing sensibility, like when adult actress August Ames was accused of homophobia with a tweet that was widely (and, I'd argue, disingenuously) misconstrued by her industry rivals.

The only solution to this is kindness and forgiveness. We need to fight our base instinct for mob justice. And we need to learn to feel sympathy and kindness for those we find fundamentally distasteful, and have done fundamentally abhorrent things. We need to rediscover our collective belief in the inherent value in human life, and that people can redeem themselves.

And if you won't do it for the wretched, perhaps do it for yourself, because who knows if you'll one day end up in the firing line of the Internet mob.

"Social Media Shaming and Forgiveness: Why Nobody's Beyond the Pale," by Matthew Hughes, The Next Web, July 5, 2019.

and do so with poise, humility, sincerity and compassion. You will see a positive return on this decision-making.

Consistently take temperature checks within the organization and outside of it with your market and society online. Think "macro" as well as "micro" when doing this, stepping outside your comfort zone into uncertainty, querying people whose response you might be uneasy about receiving.

Temperature checks, in this context, allude to people's emotions, beliefs and attitudes about you, and the intensity attached, based on the perception resulting from leadership and organizational mindset and actions. This is another risk management process and acts as insurance.

Strongly consider diversity within your inner circle—diversity of demographics as well as diversity of experiences, viewpoints and beliefs. While seeking a strong team, create room for healthy, protective conflict to best protect organizational and individual well-being.

What About Response Practices to Cancel Culture in Progress?

Don't go dark. This is a common practice. Ignoring the crisis, at least with your response to media, will prove costly; you forfeit control of the narrative—not always an accurate one, and one in which acceleration of negativity will be rapid. Many individuals and organizations have been frozen in analysis paralysis or disgust, gone dark and suffered far worse than they imagined.

Don't respond robotically. This too, is common. Having a company spokesperson or attorney speak briefly and in a wooden manner, devoid of social awareness, self-awareness, empathy and sincerity is akin to impaling your reputation on top of the adversity or crisis you are currently enduring. When you communicate, choose someone who is respected for their character and strength of humanity.

Don't respond and run. Crisis is not a one-response situation, yet that is what organizational leaders believe is safest. Communicate briefly and robotically, then disappear. This intensifies negative emotions, assumptions, beliefs, attitudes, aggression and punitive calls to action. It's predictable and earned pain if leaders choose this reckless strategy.

Humbly, patiently seek understanding. When people and groups feel understood, empathized with and recognize a sense of sincere remorse and commitment to improve a relationship, negativity and aggression often recede.

Be careful to avoid your own defensiveness or annoyance. Often in cancel culture, individuals and organizations can become emotionally triggered by negative feedback and attacks and respond with poor self-control, thereby compounding damages.

This requires suppression of ego and our own negative emotions, yet the benefits of that stress management and self-control prove protective and corrective.

Be willing to take sustained action to problem-solve to market and cultural expectations (and beyond). Words and all actions speak to and echo our beliefs, intentions and commitment. They build or deconstruct reputation. The good news is, we have a choice for building trust, restoring it, rebuilding it and benefiting, or choosing willingly to forfeit it.

Prompt, committed action to thorough, compassionate problem-solving can prevent or defuse cancel culture.

Cancel culture can largely be prevented, yet when it does emerge, and even when it hits high velocity, it can be more skillfully, successfully assessed, navigated, mitigated and problem-solved.

Periodical and Internet Sources Bibliography

The following articles have been selected to supplement the diverse views presented in this chapter.

Christopher Brito, "Cancel Culture Seems to Have Started as an Internet Joke. Now It's Anything But," CBS News, August 19, 2020. https://www.cbsnews.com/news/cancel-culture-internet -joke-anything-but/

Katie Camero, "What Is 'Cancel Culture'? J. K. Rowling Controversy Leaves Writers, Scholars Debating," *Miami Herald*, July 8, 2020. https://www.miamiherald.com/news/nation-world/national /article244082037.html

Dictionary.com, "Cancel Culture." https://www.dictionary.com/e /pop-culture/cancel-culture/

Ross Douthat, "10 Theses About Cancel Culture," *New York Times*, July 14, 2020. https://www.nytimes.com/2020/07/14/opinion /cancel-culture-.html

Susannah Goldsbrough, "Cancel Culture: What It Is, and How Did It Begin?" *Telegraph*, July 30, 2020. https://www.telegraph.co.uk /music/what-to-listen-to/cancel-culture-did-begin/

Rachel E. Greenspan, "How 'Cancel Culture' Quickly Became One of the Buzziest and Most Controversial Ideas on the Internet," *Business Insider*, August 6, 2020. https://www.insider.com/cancel -culture-meaning-history-origin-phrase-used-negatively-2020-7

Sarah Hagi, "Cancel Culture Is Not Real—At Least Not in the Way People Think," *Time*, November 21, 2019. https://time .com/5735403/cancel-culture-is-not-real/

Hillel Italie, "Everywhere and Nowhere: The Many Layers of 'Cancel Culture,'" AP News, July 26, 2020. https://apnews.com/article /nfl-george-packer-media-football-social-media-9090804abf933c 422207660509aeef22

Brooke Kato, "What Is Cancel Culture? Everything to Know About the Toxic Trend," *New York Post*, July 10, 2020. https://nypost .com/article/what-is-cancel-culture-breaking-down-the-toxic -online-trend/

Dora Mekovar, "Is Cancel Culture Killing Free Exchange of Ideas?" Voice of America, August 11, 2020. https://www.voanews.com /usa/all-about-america/cancel-culture-killing-free-exchange-ideas

Taylor Mooney and Justin Sherman, "How 'Cancel Culture' Changed These Three Lives Forever," CBS News, August 13, 2020. https:// www.cbsnews.com/news/cancel-culture-changed-lives-forever -cbsn-originals/

Aja Romano, "Why We Can't Stop Fighting About Cancel Culture," Vox, August 25, 2020. https://www.vox.com /culture/2019/12/30/20879720/what-is-cancel-culture -explained-history-debate

Brandon Tensley, "Cancel Culture Is About Power—Who Has It and Who Wants to Be Heard," CNN, July 10, 2020. https://www.cnn .com/2020/07/10/politics/cancel-culture-power/index.html

OPPOSING
VIEWPOINTS®
SERIES

CHAPTER 2

How Does Cancel Culture Affect Us?

Chapter Preface

From a sociological perspective, cancel culture can be described as how large groups of people, especially on social media platforms, tend to target those they perceive as having committed a kind of moral violation. These individuals are then often cast out of their social or professional circles.

Studies show that engaging in cancel culture increases the social status of those participating in it, and this is the primary motivation. For some, admiration from peers is more important than a sense of well-being or socioeconomic status. For social strivers, cancel culture has in essence created a new opportunity to move up socially while taking other people down.

Cancel culture is also a very social activity where people feel they are uniting behind a common purpose to take down a perpetrator. Broadcasting the misbehavior of others also offers little risk, with a high opportunity for both status and bonding with like-minded people, even if a group isn't necessarily successful in "canceling" someone.

Research published in *Psychology Today* shows that people are slow to give moral praise for good acts. Doing good and waiting for others to notice is more difficult and riskier, whereas assigning blame to others is a much easier way to achieve social status.

Finally, cancel culture produces immediate awards for people, which many prefer over avoiding the long-off possibility of future pain, even those engaged in moralizing over the nearsightedness of others. For example, the idea of preventing climate change is too long-term and overwhelming to deal with. It's much easier to address a perceived misdeed in the here and now.

The following viewpoints delve into the psychology of cancel culture and how it affects every level of society, from individual children and adults to organizations and cultures.

> "*While celebrities, successful artists, and other too-big-to-fail types can survive a cancellation (or even seek one out as a means of drumming up publicity), the rest of us are trapped in an increasingly deranged surveillance state fueled by the disappearance of our most essential resource: trust.*"

Cancel Culture Points to a Lack of Trust

Kat Rosenfield

In the following viewpoint, Kat Rosenfield examines the chilling effects cancel culture has on average people and society. While "canceling" may have started as a way to balance the power against celebrities and other people with power, it has morphed into an act of moral judgment and swift justice among average citizens. The author argues that cancel culture is not about celebrities, but about people losing trust in one another. Trust is what allows people from different walks of life to coexist. When that social trust is broken, we all live under the threat of being canceled. Kat Rosenfield is a writer who focuses on pop culture and politics and a former reporter for MTV News.

"The Real Problem with Cancel Culture," by Kat Rosenfield, October 16, 2019. This story originally appeared in *Tablet Magazine*, at tabletmag.com, and is reprinted with permission.

As you read, consider the following questions:

1. What does the author consider to be the main problem with cancel culture?
2. How does this viewpoint illustrate how cancel culture might not be real social activism?
3. How does a lack of trust invade everything, according to the author?

Of all the terms to gain prominence in 2019, few have provoked more pontification, more pearl-clutching, or more caustic dismissal than "cancel culture." Depending on where you get your discourse, you've probably already seen the phenomenon blamed on any of several culprits: technology (social media and the internet), pathology (the growing cachet of "victimhood" and its attendant incentives to claims of harm), or even one political tribe in particular ("So much for the tolerant left!"). Or, alternatively, you've heard that it's not a phenomenon at all, and that all this talk of cancellation is just the world's-tiniest-violin lament of a bunch of cultural dinosaurs, whining as they're rightly crushed into irrelevance under the wheels of progress.

But the entire cancel culture conversation, including the debate over whether or not it exists at all, has largely missed a crucial point. While celebrities, successful artists, and other too-big-to-fail types can survive a cancellation (or even seek one out as a means of drumming up publicity), the rest of us are trapped in an increasingly deranged surveillance state fueled by the disappearance of our most essential resource: trust.

In a large, diverse country, trust is the thing that keeps us living in harmony and content to let other people live as they wish, but its erosion is an institutional problem as much as an interpersonal one. Three years after Donald Trump won the presidency with promises to "drain the swamp" of untrustworthy, corrupt D.C., Americans have very little faith in the systems that keep the country running, including government, business, and media. Between

CONSEQUENCES

Cancel culture, otherwise defined as "consequences," according to a popular online joke, is a social media phenomenon wherein progressive social media users attempt to chip away at the cultural capital or professional clout of a celebrity who says or does something offensive (casteist, racist, sexist, queerphobic) by "cancelling" them.

One of the main critiques of cancel culture is that it's making people more intolerant, quick to judge and banish those who even slightly disagree with them. Critics of the cultural phenomenon say cancel culture doesn't leave any room for constructive discourse because social media users often deliver a quick verdict, based on a snap judgment, to a celebrity they perceive as offensive—leaving no opportunity for the "cancelled" person to explain themselves and make their case against their own "cancellation."

The cancel culture debate often resembles a tug of war between those trying to make room for discussion between people with opposing viewpoints and those not wanting to compromise their principles by engaging with a celebrity they view as problematic. But

2017 and 2018, trust in media, for example, dropped from 47% to 42%. Trust in government declined even more precipitously, with a 14-percentage-point drop in the number of people who said they trusted the US to "do what is right." While those numbers rebounded by a few points in 2019, Americans' overall faith in the country remained dismal: A mere 20% of Americans agreed that the system was working for them.

Meanwhile, the proliferation of fake news, along with political polarization, makes it difficult even to establish an agreed-upon set of facts from which to draw conclusions when we talk about this trust problem. We aren't sure what's real or true; we don't know who's wrong. But increasingly, we suspect that everyone is.

And that's the insidious thing about a culture where trust is eroding: A majority of people don't even have to support or participate in cancel culture for it to wreak havoc on society at people tend to forget—whether a celebrity is canceled or not is largely up to the celebrity themself, not on those wanting to cancel them.

Take Ellen DeGeneres, for example: When photos of her at a sports game with known homophobe George Bush went viral on social media, her fans started calling her out for being a hypocrite— supporting gay rights herself but also fraternizing with a former politician who actively advocated for people like DeGeneres not to have civil rights. The social media users called her out. But when DeGeneres addressed the controversy on her show, she advocated for universal kindness while herself brushing off her critics to be a bunch of over-sensitive Twitter snowflakes. Those of her fans who didn't agree with her choice to be friends with Bush realized she wasn't open to criticism, and slowly but surely, their call-outs turned to demands to cancel DeGeneres and her show. Others who didn't have much of a problem with her—this faction makes up the majority—have continued to prop up her celebrity, and she stays untouched by cancel culture.

"Cancel Culture Is Not Making People Intolerant; It's Empowering Them," by Rajvi Desai, The Swaddle, February 2, 2020.

large. In a recent *New York Times* article about political polarization, psychologist Jonathan Haidt explained how small pockets of concentrated outrage can produce immense destructive force: "You can tell me that 70 percent of Americans don't participate in the culture war, but it doesn't really matter," he wrote. "Events today are driven by small numbers that can shame and intimidate large numbers. Social media has changed the dynamic."

Haidt compares this scolding minority to arsonists, but to me, the current dynamic is more evocative of an Agatha Christie-style dinner party where all the guests are being blackmailed—or killed off one by one as punishment for their sins. Once the terrifying truth is acknowledged ("One of us in this very room is in fact the murderer!") the only safe strategy is to trust no one, and the bodies keep piling up. It doesn't matter that most people are willing to live and let live; it only takes one busy, tunneling mole to weaken our social structures to the point of collapse.

Perhaps because of the media-specific connotations of "cancellation," the cancel culture discourse often centers on art, comedy, literature, and other familiar fronts in the culture wars. But it's both bigger and more banal than that: Cancel culture is most apparent in the lives of ordinary people, who feel more powerless than ever to change the systems they feel are working against them, and for whom canceling their enemies allows the comforting illusion of control. Cancel culture is a parent combing the Facebook pages of local elementary school teachers in search of immorality (in the form of dancing, drinking, or dating) that she then reports to the superintendent—or an administrator firing a teacher after her ex-boyfriend leaks her nudes. In the latter case, the district superintendent told Lauren Miranda that she had "caused, allowed, or otherwise made it possible for a nude and/or inappropriate photograph of yourself to be distributed," by not taking "adequate precautionary measures." Translation: You shouldn't have trusted your boyfriend. You shouldn't trust anyone! Ever!

Cancel culture is a reporter digging through the Twitter history of a security guard who raised $1 million for charity to discover that he posted something racist when he was 16; it's the reporter losing his job when a thousand outraged people respond in kind; and it's also the newspaper, asked to rethink its role in enabling this sort of petty offense archaeology, instead describing the act of digging through old tweets as a routine background check: the institutionalization of mistrust happening in real time.

Cancel culture is the story of Kim Brooks, who allowed her son to wait in the car while she ran a quick errand, only to be filmed, arrested, and charged with child endangerment: not just canceled, but criminalized. For this unforgivable parenting failure (aka the thing virtually anyone born before 1990 remembers as a normal and natural part of their own childhoods), Brooks got off with a "light" sentence of community service and parenting classes—but the disruptive impact of the incident is permanent. After her arrest, Brooks wrote, "I worry that if I let my son play in the alley with the other kids and don't follow him down because there are already eight responsible adults standing around, I'll be thought of as the slacker mom who's not pulling her own. And so I accompany when I probably don't need to. I supervise and hover and interfere."

As do we all. This is how we live now, under penalty of cancellation: in a culture of screencapping, filming, and snitching. Offense-seeking and finger-pointing. It's intolerance on steroids.

It is also, unfortunately, a culture in which our petty and vindictive impulses don't just have an easy outlet in the form of social media, but where those impulses are rewarded the more we indulge them. Social media isn't just dissolving our concept of privacy; it encourages public conflict over interpersonal resolution (let alone minding your own business), and it erases the tempering effects of time, distance, or personal growth. Before social media, the stupid joke you made among friends 10 years ago would fade from memory long before it had a chance to age poorly. Now, millions of people will read and react to a tweet from 2009 as though it had been written yesterday—while Twitter's chaos-fomenting algorithm promotes the least charitable, most savage responses to the top of the heap. The result is a petri-dish environment for the internet's worst Iago types, who manipulate the fearful majority to emerge as powerful influencers (or, you know, US presidents); for the rest of us, it's as toxic as it is inescapable.

It's been more than two years since Freddie deBoer penned *Planet of Cops*, one of the first and still best analyses of the fear that feeds our current climate. Cancel culture, callout culture, cop culture: it's all the same.

"We are all informants on each other," deBoer wrote. "Contemporary political culture is an autoimmune disorder. Do you enjoy living like this? Are you not exhausted? Don't you want to break out?"

For many, clearly, the answer to that question is yes. But breaking out requires an understanding currently missing from the cancel culture conversation: The real danger is not to Dave Chappelle, Roseanne Barr, or Louis C.K. This isn't about P.C. madness, the social justice excesses that erupt on college campuses but not, for the most part, in the wider world. It's not about an insufficiently sensitive monologue on pansexuality from a pubescent cartoon character. Without trust, we become fearful and desperate to exert control. Instead of terrorism or violence or a boogeyman lurking in the bushes with a gun and a roll of duct tape, we suspect the ordinary person sitting next to us, who suspects us in return. We are less charitable, more judgmental, and more likely to go to extremes—including violence—in a quest to protect our own interests from the unknowable strangers around us, who naturally mistrust us in return. Even if you want to break that cycle, do you want to be the first? To delete the screencaps, burn the receipts, and move through the world without looking back every few steps to make sure nobody is watching; to value private resolutions over public denunciation; to go back to assuming the best of people, when you think of them at all: All of this is possible, but it will take an act of faith. Someone brave enough to not only step away from the herd, but to trust it not to trample him.

> *"Like bullying, canceling can lead to kids being isolated and ostracized. Children and adolescents are much more vulnerable than adults, and isolation can affect depressive moods, anxiety, impulsive behavior, and use of substances."*

Cancellation Limits Opportunity for Improvement

Melissa Wickes

In the following viewpont, Melissa Wickes argues that today's prevailing cancel culture can be especially confusing and damaging to children and teens. That's because kids naturally make mistakes and must be granted the opportunity to learn from their mistakes. If kids feel inhibited to express their ideas for fear of being canceled, then they won't learn how to have honest debates with people whose views differ from theirs. In addition, the social isolation that results from being canceled can have a detrimental effect on children and adolescents. Melissa Wickes is a former production editor for NY Metro Parents.

"Everything You Need to Know About Cancel Culture," by Melissa Wickes, NY Metro Parents, March 12, 2020. Reprinted by permission.

As you read, consider the following questions:

1. Why is cancel culture particularly difficult for kids and young adults?
2. What was Barrack Obama's take on cancel culture and ambiguity?
3. Is cancel culture inherently childish, according to the viewpoint?

Over the last few years, "canceling" has come up within the world of celebrities—from the #TaylorSwiftisOverParty to Louis C.K.'s banishment. But what does this really mean? To cancel is to call out a behavior—an offensive remark or an unforgiveable action—and to reject the person responsible through blocking, unfollowing, and even verbally targeting on social media platforms, according to Lizzy Duffy, senior social strategist at Sparkloft Media, a social media creative agency. Unfortunately, cancel culture is no longer just for famous people. It has made its way into classrooms and teen peer groups. And now parents are concerned it's affecting their kids. Experts are here to help you understand the implications of canceling someone and how you can help your kids cope.

What Happens When Kids Cancel Each Other

When Logan Paul, a 24-year-old YouTuber with 20.2 million subscribers, published a video that included footage of a suicide victim, people banded together to "cancel" him, which in turn pressured not only YouTube but the advertisers and sponsors he worked with to take action against him. Paul was removed from Google's Preferred, the company's premier advertising platform, which prevented him from monetizing his YouTube videos.

Teens and kids are now applying this practice to their peer groups, Duffy says. While the phrase "you're canceled" can be a joke between friends, some teens are actually boycotting classmates, and sometimes over a personal opinion.

"All the friends I had through middle school completely cut me off," a high schooler nicknamed "L" told the *New York Times*. "Ignored me, blocked me on everything, would not look at me."

When L asked a former friend why she had been isolated, she was told she was "a mooch, annoying and petty, and an emotional leech who was thirsty for validation."

When to cancel someone is an arbitrary and personal decision. As Arielle Rokhsar, a junior at the Wheatley School in Old Westbury, explains: "There is no definite line between what actions allow for one to be canceled and for one to be spared. It all depends on how the audience interprets it."

And values are constantly evolving. Ali Bhalloo, Arielle's classmate, argues the "views that we have today may be considered wrong in the future. Opinions change with time. In my opinion, it is crucial that we cancel culture."

The Psychological Impact of Canceling

Like bullying, canceling can lead to kids being isolated and ostracized, says Rebecca Sinclair, Ph.D., child and adolescent psychologist and director of psychological services at Brooklyn Minds, a mental health practice with locations in Brooklyn, Manhattan, and Manhasset. "Children and adolescents are much more vulnerable than adults, and isolation can affect depressive moods, anxiety, impulsive behavior, and use of substances."

Plus, cancellation can make individuals afraid to stand up for themselves or voice an opinion, says Alexandra Hamlet, Psy.D., clinical psychologist in the Mood Disorders Center at the Child Mind Institute, a nonprofit that helps children and families with mental health and learning disorders. She says that while there are instances when avoidance can be appropriate—such as when someone is racist or harassing—it's always better to first have a discussion with the individual and help him understand that what was said is not okay.

CANCEL CULTURE AT A STATE UNIVERSITY

Thanks to social media platforms like Twitter and Facebook, regular everyday people have greater opportunities than ever to share their opinions. Opinion leaders can be anyone now and in recent years, who gained the power to "cancel" someone for saying or doing anything deemed controversial.

According to Urban Dictionary, cancel culture is when a person is stripped of their status due to accusations, whether or not they have merit.

Not only can cancel culture affect celebrities, but students and staff as well. If there is any situation brought to attention on social media, individuals involved can be called out online and brought to a negative light. This calling-out process provides unnecessary observation to people who might not have wanted attention in the first place. A hostile online environment ensues, creating bigger effects than expected.

Earlier this year, the Texas State Student Government decided to bar a conservative group on campus, Turning Point USA. The leader of the group posted a video that went viral depicting protesting

"A question that should be asked is, 'does the person really deserve the removal of support in such a reactive way for saying one thing that might have been disagreed with?'" Dr. Hamlet says.

Some Issues with Cancellation

A community that unites against someone who has done something unforgivable can be empowering. It can also make kids think twice before posting or announcing potentially offensive views.

But there's a negative too. "It's balancing this fine line because we want to give our youth and teens the opportunity and power to call [them] out when there are issues in teen behavior," Dr. Sinclair students, who were thought to be liberal, as harmful people. The video quickly spread, gaining attention from thousands of people, including Gov. Greg Abbott.

Because of the video, students' faces were now glued to all feeds about Texas State and student politics. Republican and conservative students painted the image students were violent on campus.

Due to cancel culture, comedians and speakers may struggle to find a campus to perform. During a segment of Vice news, bookers for college campuses mentioned if students do not like or agree with one thing a performer says, they can tell the entertainer to change their set.

The bookers make these calls to preserve the campus image and protect students. However, if a student does not like one joke or deems it "inappropriate," they have the right to not let the performer give a show at all.

Cancel culture does not just stick faces to a bad image but makes people feel bad for liking or agreeing with certain things.

"Cancel Culture Is Toxic," by Delilah Alvarado, *The University Star*, December 2, 2019.

points out. "The issue is, [cancellation] doesn't leave opportunity for improvement."

People—especially kids—make mistakes. Kids have not had as many experiences to learn from as adults have. Learning from failures allows adolescents to build up social skills, develop a sense of self, and develop a sense of relationships, Dr. Sinclair says.

In 2019, President Barack Obama disparaged the concept of canceling someone in an interview about youth activism. "The world is messy. There are ambiguities," he said. "People who do really good stuff have flaws. People who you are fighting may love their kids and share certain things with you."

And kids are often not told they've been canceled, or the reason behind it. A confrontation would at least provide them with an opportunity to apologize, learn, and grow, Duffy says.

Dr. Sinclair also points out that the confusion caused by social isolation often causes teens to become defensive and cling onto the opinion or belief that led to the cancellation in the first place.

Parents' Roles in Cancel Culture

Like any other difficult conversation with your adolescent, it is important to understand where your child is coming from.

"Cancel culture might make the parent really uncomfortable and alert them in a hyper-vigilant way, but it is important to hear from the kids what their emotion and experience is, whether it's worry, sadness, or anger," Dr. Sinclair says. "There can be a difference between validating a child's emotion and agreeing with their behaviors. You can validate how frustrated they are and how confused they are without agreeing that canceling someone is the right thing."

Also, as Duffy points out, cancel culture makes it difficult for adolescents to have transparent conversations about things they disagree about, which is an important life skill.

Dr. Hamlet suggests parents focus on teaching their child what it means to understand someone else's point of view and that settling differences doesn't have to mean blocking someone out of your life or unfollowing them on social media.

> *"Cancel Culture curbs public discourse and creates echo chambers. A 1996 MIT study prophetically predicted that the internet would lead to more echo chambers, areas of conversation in which no differing views are expressed."*

Cancel Culture Harms All of Society

T. J. Roberts

In the following viewpoint, T. J. Roberts argues that cancel culture is an ineffective means of seeking justice or effecting change. Instead, it shuts down the avenue toward discussion and understanding because the "canceled" parties do not have a chance to explain or redeem themselves. According to the author, cancel culture is a method of control, particularly when political correctness fails. The result is the destruction of individual thoughts and ideas in favor of a mob mentality. T. J. Roberts was a participant in the 2019 Ron Paul Scholars Seminar.

"Cancel Culture: Its Causes and Its Consequences," by T. J. Roberts, Advocates for Self-Government, February 24, 2020. Reprinted by permission.

As you read, consider the following questions:

1. Why is cancel culture not about accountability, according to the author?
2. How does the author compare political correctness to fascism?
3. What is an echo chamber, with respect to cancel culture?

The Cancel Culture Mob knows few limitations. While social media has empowered people to speak their minds, it has also empowered the masses to attempt to "cancel" those who express controversial opinions. Victims of cancel culture often end up jobless, friendless, and helpless.

Those engaging in canceling people, however, gain nothing but empty satisfaction. In a Cancel Culture, everyone loses the ability to understand differing perspectives, making echo chambers and their disastrous consequences inevitable.

What Is Cancel Culture?

Cancel Culture has been described as accountability by its proponents, but that is not a fair assessment of this phenomenon. If Cancel Culture implied accountability, then there would be an avenue for redemption. When the mob controls justice, there is no means by which you can regain their respect.

In the research paper "Does Apologizing Work? An Empirical Test of the Conventional Wisdom," Richard Hanania of Columbia University shows that public apologies typically have no effect or make the mob want the offender to be punished even more. In other words, Cancel Culture is not about Accountability.

Jeff Deist, president of the Mises Institute, provides a great definition: "Cancel culture means shutting people out of jobs, opportunities, platforms, & social settings—attempting to impoverish people, financially and otherwise." The point of Cancel Culture rests in the name—eliminating thought criminals from polite society. If the mob cannot control what you say, they will attempt to control your ability to function in society. To put it another way, Cancel Culture is the necessary tactic the mob adopts when the conventional tactics of Political Correctness fails.

Weaponized Political Correctness

Jeff Deist defines Political Correctness as "the conscious, designed manipulation of language intended to change the way people speak, write, think, feel, and act, in furtherance of an agenda." The goal of PC is to shape modern humanity into something that goes against our very nature. It destroys individualism and distinct communities and replaces our nature with mob-imposed values. It is not about good manners; it is about control.

But what happens when people refuse to be controlled? What happens when the programming fails? When people push back against PC, the mob must resort to more drastic measures. In the same way fascism emerged as a socialist's last resort to impose their unnatural worldview, Cancel Culture emerged as a means to achieve a politically correct society. If you do not bend your knee to the mob, then the mob will unperson you.

This works remarkably well against ordinary people. But with someone like Michael Bloomberg, a billionaire who imposed racist "Stop-and-Frisk" upon millions of people, there is no way to cancel him. Bloomberg's money and financial connections shield him from being canceled. Those engaged in Cancel Culture do not fight for justice. Rather, they target vulnerable individuals and preclude them from ever redeeming themselves (assuming what they said was actually wrong). Rather than have a conversation with people who hold different opinions, the Cancel Culture mob would prefer to dehumanize their adversaries.

The Consequences

Cancel Culture not only harms individuals who fall in the mob's crosshairs, it harms all of society. When you hold a view that the PC Mob may disagree with, the Herd Psychology of the canceler imposes fear upon your psyche. Because of this fear, you either don't express your opinion or you only express your opinion around people you know to agree with you. In other words, Cancel Culture curbs public discourse and creates echo chambers. A 1996 MIT study prophetically predicted that the internet would lead to more echo chambers, areas of conversation in which no differing views are expressed.

This study indicated that echo chambers lead to increased radicalization and decreased understanding of the "other side." In a study on links between echo chambers, radicalism, and violence, Nature Research indicates that such an atmosphere is a breeding ground for violence. People internalize their beliefs. Rather than you believing in your politics, you become your politics. If someone disagrees with your perspective, they do so with ill will according to PC culture. Society confirms this grim prediction as people become more hostile about their politics. Radical organizations like Antifa and other groups engage in violence against their political opponents. To lay it bare, politics drops its pretenses and exposes itself as the violent struggle it truly is.

Cancel Culture benefits no one. Rather, it gives a false sense of dispute resolution and gives the "canceler" a false sense of improved social status while isolating people from civil society. The time to fight back is now. First, refuse to "cancel" anyone. Don't engage in the mob's tactics. Talk with people with whom you disagree. Second, engage in alternative media. The State Linguistic Complex has its filthy fingers in all mainstream media. Provide your own counter-narrative. Tell the Truth. Unless we fight back against Political Correctness and Cancel Culture, discourse will die.

"If you want to support a city that has been bombed, don't think a hashtag is going to solve anything. Send them money, food and clothing. To make a difference in the world, you have to stop thinking a trending word on social media is going to accomplish anything without a plan."

Hashtag Activism Is a Start

Donah Mbabazi and Joan Mbabazi

In the following viewpoint, Donah Mbabazi and Joan Mbabazi examine the efficacy of hashtag activism or social justice campaigns in the larger context of cancel culture. It has been noted that cancel culture got its start with hashtag activism movements such as #MeToo and #BlackLivesMatter and grew on internet platforms from there. The authors argue that while hashtags can be effective in reaching a large number of people relatively quickly with very little effort, they also do not guarantee results. Real advocacy requires funding, strategies, and action plans in addition to raising awareness. Donah Mbabazi and Joan Mbabazi are journalists based in Rwanda.

As you read, consider the following questions:

1. What is the difference between positive and negative hashtag activism?
2. What are the limits of hashtag activism, according to the viewpoint?
3. Why do some activists believe social justice warriors on the internet are not real activists?

People and organisations are using social media to spread ideas and gain support for their causes at exceptional levels. Memorable movements like #BringBackOurGirls, #MeToo and #BlackLivesMatter have seen wide international coverage in the past years.

Like many things, activism has evolved; there were, and still are, physical protests held by prominent figures—the likes of Malcom X and Martin Luther King Jr in the past—to online advocacy using social media platforms like Twitter and Facebook under the use of a hashtag.

Hashtag activism is a term coined by media outlets which refers to the use of Twitter's hashtags for online activism. The term can also be used to refer to the act of showing support for a cause through a like, share, and etcetera, on any social media platform, such as Facebook or Twitter.

The term is used to refer to the use of hashtags on multiple social media platforms to plan marches and protests, share stories, connect communities, and ultimately, drive social change.

The Launch of the Hashtag

The concept of tagging social media groups or topics with a hashtag is credited to one man, Chris Messina, who came up with the idea in 2007.

He got the idea of using a hashtag from online chat rooms. He decided to pitch the idea to Twitter, but the company told him it was "nerdy" and that it would never catch on.

He did not give up. Instead, he started asking friends to give the hashtag a try.

In October of 2007, one of his friends was tweeting about a San Diego wildfire. Messina asked him to add #sandiegofire to his tweets. It didn't take long for others to start using the same hashtag.

The idea caught on, and in 2009 Twitter added an option for users to search for hashtags.

Instagram launched it in 2010 and Facebook in 2013.

While some users simply want to brag on social media, others are using the versatile tool for change. #NeverAgain, #MeToo and #BlackLivesMatter movements have gained incredible momentum thanks to their hashtags.

Many believe that tweeting or posting information online is an effective form of advocacy. But does this sort of activism really have an effect on the world? Or are users just blowing smoke?

What Is the Impact?

Ashley Rudo Chisamba, a gender activist, admits to being a big supporter of hashtag activism and thinks it's effective for many reasons.

One, it is pocket friendly; different from other activism campaigns that entail t-shirts or banners which can be expensive. You can make an impact or influence an action with little, she says.

Chisamba also says that an individual can start a movement without necessarily needing a crowd to kick-start the campaign.

"It is different from real live activism which is normally dependent on numbers. Hashtag activism enables one to start a movement, and it can grow beyond your social circle; a big population of the world is on social media," she says.

Chisamba notes that this form of activism enables wide outreach because it raises awareness on issues that ordinary activism may restrict to a situation, citing the #JusticeforBankMom, a hashtag started by one activist after seeing a woman being abused in a bank in Ghana. It spread like wildfire to the point of attracting the attention of authorities, including the President of Ghana, who arrested the perpetrators and ensured that justice was exercised in the matter.

The world is also evolving and most government authorities, police, ministries and even Presidents' offices are on Twitter—these are offices ordinary people cannot access easily. Hashtag activism enables people to access such platforms and create movements around them, Chisamba adds.

"I strongly believe that as the world is evolving, hashtag activism is the future, it has good examples of impact. Most hashtag campaigns have moved on to being adopted across the globe, bringing more voice and urgency to important issues, a good example is #BringBackOurGirls."

Pamela Mudakikwa, a communications officer, says that hashtags can cause a great movement in fighting for change and awareness on different issues, but only if they are positive.

She says when you form negative hashtags, they can create a negative impact on someone's image or organisation, which might also demolish the purpose of which they are formed.

However, she notes that for online activism to be effective, activists should talk about a cause that attracts people. That way, the hashtag can easily be shared on different social media platforms.

"Hashtags can be effective if they are short and easy to understand, they can only attract a wider audience if people can easily grasp them," Mudakikwa explains.

Bobby Rutarindwa, a social media enthusiast and blogger, says hashtags can be effective in the sense that they create solidarity to achieve a common goal.

He emphasises that hashtags can be effective in promoting activism when they have a clear vision that many people can relate to.

"Most of them fail because they are controversial and have a goal to destabilise societies, rather than building them before you form a hashtag, arranging it, knowing who it is for, and the purpose you are forming it, and letting it have a clear objective," Rutarindwa says.

Is Online Activism Masked Outrage?

Moise Kabera, a social media user, says though this kind of activism can be initiated with pure motives, some people who take part either by sharing or promoting the tweets or tags do it for the sake of it and do not really care about the cause.

"Some people just want to appear trendy and seem as though they care yet in real sense they want to be part of a trending topic, this means little or no success for such activism," he says.

Ninnette Umuhoza agrees with Kabera saying that the former way of activism is more effective because matters handled online are easily ignored, which is not the case with physical activism.

"With the speed at which technology is moving, millions of people use social media which leads to trends changing in seconds, and the minute a new one comes up, the other is forgotten. I don't think such platforms are the best way of doing activism," she says.

Umuhoza also thinks that the determination it takes to start a physical movement is what makes it effective, otherwise when it comes to online platforms, anyone with an idea is free to post what they want.

Author Sara Lippert says in her article "Hashtag Activism: Is It Effective, Lazy, or Selfish?" the issue with hashtag activism is whether or not it is actually making a difference in the world, or if it is just a way for people to feel like they are making a difference.

Just because the whole world knows about a problem or acknowledges that it exists doesn't mean that the problem is fixed. Actions need to be taken in order to fix the problem, and most would say that adding a hashtag to social media isn't an effective action, bringing about the term "slacktivism."

For issues such as world hunger, using #hunger isn't going to solve anything other than raise awareness. Just because a hashtag is trending doesn't mean the issue is being dealt with, she notes.

Lippert goes on to write that it is possible for hashtag activism to be effective. However, other than creating awareness, most campaigns don't seem to make an actual impact. Some use the hashtags to bring attention to themselves in the midst of what's often a tragedy. They use the hashtags to be thought well of as a compassionate or involved person.

She points out that success isn't measured by how many times a hashtag is used, rather, by how much it truly helped the situation. The best way to make a hashtag activism campaign effective is to have a call to action. It needs money for the cause. It needs a doable plan to resolve the issue.

If you want to support a city that has been bombed, don't think a hashtag is going to solve anything. Send them money, food and clothing. To make a difference in the world, you have to stop thinking a trending word on social media is going to accomplish anything without a plan. So instead, volunteer your time. Volunteer your money and donate to charities. Send your prayers out to those in need. But never rely solely on a hashtag to save the world, Lippert writes.

> *"Using social media or the Internet to attack people you disagree with isn't 'activism' no matter what impact it has on your own sense of moral superiority."*

Cancel Culture Doesn't Accomplish Anything

Doug Mataconis

In the following viewpoint, Doug Mataconis reports on remarks made by Barack Obama regarding cancel culture. Speaking to youth activists, the former president cautioned that "wokeness" by way of hashtag activism does not go very far if there are no actions to back it up. Obama cited the work of activists Dr. Martin Luther King Jr and John Lewis during the civil rights era in the United States as examples of activism that actually effects change. The author contends that the wholsesale canceling of people for being different degrees of offensive fails to take into consideration the complexities of the human race. Doug Mataconis is a staff writer for Outside the Beltway.

"Obama Calls Out 'Woke' Culture," by Doug Mataconis, *Outside the Beltway*, November 5, 2019. Reprinted by permission. https://www.outsidethebeltway.com/obama-calls-out-woke-culture/

As you read, consider the following questions:

1. Why does President Obama say the world is messy?
2. In what ways can change really be made, according to the viewpoint?
3. According to the author, who supported Obama's remarks?

Former President Barack Obama spoke out last week about so-called "wokeness," or what he called "call-out culture," asserting that it isn't real activism and that it isn't accomplishing anything:

Former President Barack Obama made a rare foray into the cultural conversation this week, objecting to the prevalence of "call-out culture" and "wokeness" during an interview about youth activism at the Obama Foundation summit on Tuesday.

For more than an hour, Mr. Obama sat onstage with the actress Yara Shahidi and several other young leaders from around the world. The conversation touched on "leadership, grass roots change and the power places have to shape our journeys," the Obama Foundation said, but it was his remarks about young activists that have ricocheted around the internet, mostly receiving praise from a cohort of bipartisan and intergenerational supporters.

"This idea of purity and you're never compromised and you're always politically 'woke' and all that stuff," Mr. Obama said. "You should get over that quickly."

"The world is messy; there are ambiguities," he continued. "People who do really good stuff have flaws. People who you are fighting may love their kids, and share certain things with you."

Mr. Obama spoke repeatedly of the role of social media in activism specifically, including the idea of what's become known as "cancel culture," which is much remarked upon, but still nebulously defined. It tends to refer to behavior that mostly plays out on the internet when someone has said or done something to which others object. That person is then condemned in a flurry of social media posts. Such people are often referred to as "canceled," a way of saying that many others (and perhaps the places at which they work) are fed up with them and will have no more to do with them.

Mr. Obama talked about conversations he's had with his daughter Malia, who is a student at Harvard with Ms. Shahidi.

"I do get a sense sometimes now among certain young people, and this is accelerated by social media, there is this sense sometimes of: 'The way of me making change is to be as judgmental as possible about other people,'" he said, "and that's enough."

"Like, if I tweet or hashtag about how you didn't do something right or used the wrong verb," he said, "then I can sit back and feel pretty good about myself, cause, 'Man, you see how woke I was, I called you out.'"

Then he pretended to sit back and press the remote to turn on a television.

"That's not activism. That's not bringing about change," he said. "If all you're doing is casting stones, you're probably not going to get that far. That's easy to do."

The former President's comments brought about rare agreement across the political and cultural aisles:

Former president Barack Obama offered some advice earlier this week to young people hoping to change society: participating in cancel culture isn't the way to do it.

"This idea of purity and you're never compromised and you're always politically woke and all that stuff, you should get over that quickly," the 58-year-old said Tuesday while speaking at the Obama Foundation Summit in Chicago. "The world is messy. There are ambiguities. People who do really good stuff have flaws."

Obama's pointed warning that social media enables "woke" people to be "as judgmental as possible" went viral Wednesday, drawing praise from both the left and right. By early Thursday, clips of Obama shared on Twitter had been viewed millions of times as many stressed that all social media users needed to hear his message.

"He is right on all counts," 2020 Democratic presidential candidate Andrew Yang tweeted, while his opponent Rep. Tulsi Gabbard (D-Hawaii) wrote, "We all need a little more aloha spirit—being respectful & caring for one another."

"Good for Obama," wrote conservative pundit Ann Coulter, adding in parentheses that her comment was "Not sarcastic!"

On Tuesday, Obama was roughly 50 minutes into a discussion with young leaders about their activism when he mentioned that he had started to notice a worrisome trend "among young people, particularly on college campuses."

"There is this sense sometimes of, 'The way of me making change is to be as judgmental as possible about other people,' and that's enough," he said, noting that the mind-set was only "accelerated by social media."

Obama went on to describe an example of the behavior he was cautioning against.

(…)

Obama effectively inserted himself into the ongoing debate that surrounds cancel culture, a term that refers to a mass effort, usually carried out on social media, to call out prominent people for any alleged wrongdoing and demand that they lose access to their public platforms. The strategy has proved vital to holding powerful figures accountable, sparking international movements such as #MeToo. But "canceling" has also been criticized for encouraging mob behavior that often results in major consequences to people's lives and careers over missteps such as old inappropriate tweets, The *Washington Post*'s Abby Ohlheiser and Elahe Izadi reported.

Boycotts have long been considered an efficient method of motivating change, but the intense censoring of people or groups on social media is a newer tactic that has gained popularity on the left over the past several years, according to CNN's Chris Cillizza, who described it as "one of the defining hallmarks of our culture in the post-Obama presidency."

"Say something wrong, tweet something people disagree with, express an opinion that is surprising or contradicts the established view people have of you, and the demands for you to be fired, de-friended or otherwise driven from the realms of men quickly follow," Cillizza wrote.

It is not especially surprising then that Obama, known for promoting compromise, would take issue with an approach that hinges on the premise that everything is black and white—and Tuesday wasn't the first time that he has publicly raised concerns. In his first interview after leaving office, Obama criticized unnamed leaders for using social media to sow division, the *Post*'s William Booth reported.

While conservatives will complain that it is solely something that has arisen on the left from what they refer to as "social justice warriors," the truth of the matter that using social media to call out or attempt to intimidate people on the opposite side is something that both sides of the political aisle have engaged in. All it takes is for someone, and in particular, a celebrity or political figure to say something controversial publicly or on social media and the wolves start to circle demanding their piece of flesh. Sometimes it's something as seemingly inconsequential as trying to get you banned from one social media platform or another, although it's worth noting that for some people that alone can have a significant impact on their ability to do their job. On other occasions, it expands to include demands that the alleged wrongdoer be fired from their jobs.

If you ask the people who engage in this kind of activity, they'll tell you that they're in engaging in "activism" in "calling out" people who have said or done offensive but not illegal things in the past. The truth, though, is somewhere closer to what President Obama said. Using social media or the Internet to attack people you disagree with isn't "activism" no matter what impact it has on your own sense of moral superiority, In fact, one could argue that it's not activism but laziness. Activism means getting out into the world and trying to change it by registering voters, attending rallies, and effect change.

Using your Twitter account and a hashtag to harass someone who crosses a line is easy, involves no sacrifices, and doesn't really require any real work. The only thing such "activism" accomplishes is to make the people who engage in it feel like they accomplished something by just coming up with a clever tweet or Facebook post, and putting the phone back down and returning to whatever show you happen to be streaming on Netflix. It allows you to show your friends and the world how "woke" you are without actually engaging in anything productive or engaging in the kind of action that people such as Martin Luther King, John Lewis, and the civil rights protesters of the 1950s and 1960s engaged in.

So far at least, I haven't seen any blowback directed at the former President for what he said, and perhaps it's possible that his words will have an impact. As he said, not only is the whole idea of "call-out culture" anathema to what activism is really all about but it goes against the realities of a nation where few people are unambiguously good or evil. Attacking people and demanding that they be fired because of something they said in the past accomplishes nothing except, as I said, feeding one's own self-satisfied sense of superiority at no cost.

Periodical and Internet Sources Bibliography

The following articles have been selected to supplement the diverse views presented in this chapter.

Delilah Alvarado, "Cancel Culture Is Toxic," *University Star*, December 2, 2019. https://www.universitystar.com/opinions /cancel-culture-is-toxic/article_6e256b21-2d51-5846-ac31 -9312bb5789ce.html

Phoebe Maltz Bovy, "Cancel Culture Is a Real Problem. But Not for the People Warning About It," *Washington Post*, July 9, 2020. https://www.washingtonpost.com/outlook/2020/07/09/cancel -culture-is-real-problem-not-people-warning-about-it/

John Burton, "The Outrage Mob: Shame, Bullying and Social Abuse in America's Cancel Culture," *Stream*, June 12, 2020. https:// stream.org/the-outrage-mob-shame-bullying-and-social-abuse -in-americas-cancel-culture/

Alexandra D'Amour, "Cancel Culture: The Good, the Bad & Its Impact on Social Change," On Our Moon, retrieved September 15, 2020. https://onourmoon.com/cancel-culture-the-good-the -bad-its-impact-on-social-change/

Victoria Diaz, "You're Cancelled! Cancel Culture as a Tool for Bullying and Harassment," *Science Survey*, March 18, 2020. https://thesciencesurvey.com/editorial/2020/03/18/youre -cancelled-cancel-culture-as-a-tool-for-bullying-and-harassment/

Lindsay Dodgson, "The Frenzy of Unrelenting Online Bullying Further Destroys the Mental Health of Those Already Suffering, and Everyone Has a Role to Play," *Insider*, February 25, 2020. https://static1.insider.com/toxic-tragic-results-of-online-hate -bullying-cancel-culture-2020-2

Lesley Hauler, "I Was Canceled and It Nearly Destroyed My Life," *Good Morning America*, January 17, 2020. https://www .goodmorningamerica.com/living/story/canceled-destroyed -life-68311913

Robert Henderson, "The Atavism of Cancel Culture," *City Journal*, September 30, 2019. https://www.city-journal.org/cancel-culture

The Learning Network, "What Students Are Saying About Cancel Culture, Friendly Celebrity Battles and Finding Escape," *New York Times*, November 19, 2020. https://www.nytimes .com/2020/11/19/learning/what-students-are-saying-about -cancel-culture-friendly-celebrity-battles-and-finding-escape. html

NBC Bay Area, "Cancel Culture: How to Stop Accountability from Becoming Bullying," August 12, 2020. https://www.nbcbayarea .com/lx/cancel-culture-how-to-stop-accountability-from -turning-into-bullying/2343223/

Procon.org, "Is Cancel Culture (or Callout Culture) Good for Society?" August 5, 2020. https://www.procon.org/headlines /is-cancel-culture-or-callout-culture-good-for-society/

What Social Problems
Does Cancel Culture
Highlight?

Chapter Preface

The cancel culture conversation—and even the debate over its existence at all—may miss the point on how it is impacting our society. It's been pointed out that celebrities and other people in the spotlight can survive a cancellation and even use it to their advantage by creating publicity around themselves. However, average everyday people and those whose careers and lives can be damaged find themselves deprived of an essential ingredient of public life—that of trust.

Trust in our institutions has suffered greatly in the past four or five years, especially with the controversial election and governance of Donald Trump. People now have little faith in systems that keep our daily lives running. As an example, trust in the media is now at only 42 percent, according to some polls. Americans have less trust in government, business, and the journalists bringing us news than ever before.

The rise of social media, while expanding communications as a whole, also has everyone questioning reality more than ever before. Increasing political polarization makes it difficult to establish agreed-upon facts when the issue of lack of trust is raised. Writers who explore cancel culture often concentrate on culture wars: art, comedy, sports, drama, or literature. But cancel culture is very much present in the lives of average people who, feeling unable to enact change in the systems they feel are not working for them, find the canceling of their "enemies" an illusory control.

Cancel culture is that friend on Facebook who finds it necessary to nail you to the cross for discrepancies in the "correct" opinion, banning you from their pages. Cancel culture is parents concerned about the morality of schoolteachers, searching online for evidence for their kid's teacher's Twitter account. Cancel culture is being scared you will make any ideological mistake in the face of absolute certainty. And you will know that it is cancel culture because it creates an atmosphere of fear.

> *"It's happened to pretty much every woman you know. I think it's really important that we don't allow this to become a story about this one bad guy who did these terrible things because he's a monster … it happens in every country every day to all women."*

Social Media Made It Easier to Highlight the Sexual Misconduct of Powerful Men

Nadia Khomami

In the following viewpoint, Nadia Khomami details the beginnings of the #MeToo movement online, which can be credited for the arrest and conviction of Hollywood mogul Harvey Weinstein for using his position of power to sexually assault and sexually abuse women over the course of decades. It also brought global focus to the issue of sexual harassment and sexual abuse, which, it became painfully clear, is all too ubiquitous in society, not only in Hollywood. Nadia Khomami is the assistant news editor at the Guardian.

As you read, consider the following questions:

1. Allegations against what Hollywood producer catapulted the #MeToo movement?
2. When did #MeToo begin?
3. What is a "whisper network"?

It started with an exposé detailing countless allegations against Hollywood producer Harvey Weinstein. But soon, personal stories began pouring in from women in all industries across the world, and the hashtag #MeToo became a rallying cry against sexual assault and harassment.

The movement began on social media after a call to action by the actor Alyssa Milano, one of Weinstein's most vocal critics, who wrote: "If all the women who have been sexually harassed or assaulted wrote 'Me too' as a status, we might give people a sense of the magnitude of the problem."

Within days, millions of women—and some men—used Twitter, Facebook and Instagram to disclose the harassment and abuse they have faced in their own lives. They included celebrities and public figures such as Björk and Olympic gymnast McKayla Maroney, as well as ordinary people who felt empowered to finally speak out. The story moved beyond any one man; it became a conversation about men's behaviour towards women and the imbalance of power at the top.

Mhairi Black, the MP for Paisley and Renfrewshire South, said it made for harrowing reading: "Even on my personal Facebook, stories are coming up, and it's 'My God, I didn't know that had happened' … It's brilliant that women are coming forward and I'm sick to the back teeth especially of other women saying 'you should have said something long ago.' Don't dare put that on folk. The exact reason that they're speaking out now is to make sure that the next generation don't have to feel the way they did. I think it's really harrowing reading through it."

Nearly 68,000 people have so far replied to Milano's tweet, and the #MeToo hashtag has been used more than 1m times in the US, Europe, the Middle East and beyond. The French used #balancetonporc, the Spanish #YoTambien, and in Arab countries the hashtags أنا_كمان# and أنا_ايضا# were predominant.

Facebook said that within 24 hours, 4.7 million people around the world engaged in the #MeToo conversation, with over 12m posts, comments, and reactions.

"It is about so much more than Harvey Weinstein," said Caroline Criado-Perez, co-founder of the Women's Room and the feminist campaigner who forced the Bank of England to have female representation on banknotes.

"That's what #MeToo represents, it's happened to pretty much every woman you know. I think it's really important that we don't allow this to become a story about this one bad guy who did these terrible things because he's a monster, and to make it clear that actually, it's not just monsters … it happens in every country every day to all women, and it's done by friends, colleagues, 'good guys' who care about the environment and children and even feminism, supposedly."

The origins of #MeToo can be dated back before the predominance of social media, when activist Tarana Burke created the campaign as a grass-roots movement to reach sexual assault survivors in underprivileged communities.

"It has been amazing watching all of the pushback against Harvey Weinstein and in support of his accusers over the last week," Burke wrote. "In particular, today I have watched women on social media disclose their stories … it made my heart swell to see women using this idea."

The internet age has better equipped people to deal with these issues. Social media has democratised feminism, helping women to share experiences of sexual violence, such as on the HarassMap platform launched in Egypt, build solidarity, as seen with the #YesAllWomen hashtag that trended for weeks after Elliot Rodger went on a shooting spree in California, or keep international attention on events that slipped off the news agenda, such as the #BringBackOurGirls campaign launched after the abduction of more than 300 schoolgirls in Chibok, Nigeria.

"I don't think we [should] underestimate how much of an impact is being made by the way in which women can just speak out about their experiences, because we're just not represented in the news media, and films and literature," said Criado-Perez. "Until the internet came along, we just weren't having these conversations about what it's like to be a woman, what it's like to walk down the street and be harassed and cat-called. We didn't know about the idea of everyday sexism."

The movement is part of a string of hashtags and methods used by women to highlight harassment. The Weinstein revelations also came on the anniversary of the leaked 2005 Access Hollywood tape, in which Donald Trump bragged about kissing and touching women because "when you're a star, they let you do it." At the time, the writer Kelly Oxford said she received millions of Twitter interactions when she encouraged women to share their own experiences using the hashtag #NotOkay.

Then there has been the rise of "whisper networks," unofficial channels women use to warn each other about creepy or even criminal men. An anonymously created Google spreadsheet was passed around, listing "shitty media men," accused of everything from sending inappropriate direct messages to violent sexual assault. Growing numbers of women, using various platforms, are having private conversations about the "open-secret" reputations of men in their industry.

The effects are being seen every day. One anonymous woman used the #MeToo hasthag to accuse Vice journalist Sam Kriss of forcibly kissing and harassing her. Kriss posted an apology on Medium, but has since been sacked from Vice and had his membership to the Labour party suspended. On Thursday, British GQ's political correspondent, Rupert Myers, was also fired after a number of women made allegations against him on Twitter. The next day, Vox Media's editorial director, Lockhart Steele, was fired over allegations made against him in a Medium post.

The movement has also inspired a series of offshoot hashtags used by men, including #IDidThat and #HowIWillChange, in which men have admitted inappropriate behaviour.

> *"Yet, it's the myth of cancel culture that has earned it such an unsatisfactory veneer. This idea that if, say, Bill Cosby or Logan Paul or Doja Cat was cancelled, it was done so in a rush to judgment. But cancellation does not imply moralism, or heedless impulse—it only requires that we reckon with the truth as it is."*

Cancellation Is an Act of Catharsis

Jason Parham

In the following viewpoint, Jason Parham argues that cancel culture is the culture of rebellion and an act of catharsis. The author uses rapper Kanye West as a vehicle to explore celebrity behavior and cancellation. While cancel culture is often criticized as little more than a purity test, cancellation is actually a reckoning, a collective acknowledgment that we can no longer accept a certain person's behavior, according to Parnham. In the end, the author decides that while perhaps West does not merit cancellation, neither does he deserve infinite chances, based on his long-term behavior. Jason Parham is a senior writer at Wired, *where he covers popular culture.*

"The Devolution of Kanye West and the Case for Cancel Culture," by Jason Parham, *Wired* c/o Condé Nast, May 5, 2018. Reprinted by permission.

As you read, consider the following questions:

1. Why does the author believe Kanye West should be canceled?
2. What two opposing pieces of West's clothing does the author describe as a way of illustrating the singer's competing messages?
3. As a former fan, what is the author's conclusion about West?

Kanye West wants to be "a channel of light and love to the world." According to a recent statement he posted to Twitter, the rapper-provocateur believes "Love based intention and action creates more love, joy, happiness, and abundance in your life." It's a bizarrely confounding admission from the Grammy-winning artist—not for its message, but for the irritatingly paradoxical actions of its trigger-happy, say-anything messenger.

For both fans and ardent critics of West, the weeks preceding the post proved a high-wire act of drama and misinformation displaying all the pages in the Kanye playbook. There were the outbursts: standing on a desk, he railed at Detroit college students about Elon Musk's alleged stock fraud, "Leave that man the f**k alone!" There were the retrogressive avowals: absurdly dressing as a sparkling water bottle for a performance of the spastic "I Love It," followed by a rambling post-show speech in which he cast himself as the victim of ideological bullying and per SNL cast member Kenan Thompson, proceeded to "caca on people." And of course, there were the high-volume, low-context proclamations he's become famous for: press stops that included grossly inaccurate statements about slavery, including the desire to abolish the 13th Amendment (which he later clarified in a futile effort to criticize America's prison system). Finally, perhaps expectedly, the majority ruling landed with abrupt justice: Kanye West is cancelled.

Another Celebrity Canceling

A few months ago, the internet latched onto its latest controversy: Kevin Hart's old tweets. In his posts from 2009 to 2011, Hart made homophobic comments and used derogatory language towards the gay community. The tweets resurfaced after the announcement that Hart would host the 2019 Oscars.

After the tweets began circulating, Hart tweeted a short apology for his "insensitive words" and stated that he would step down from hosting the show. The Academy asked the comedian to issue a formal apology to regain his spot, but Hart declined, claiming that he did not want to "feed the internet trolls" that shamed him for his earlier social media posts.

I found myself troubled for two reasons after seeing the situation unfold, the first being that I thought it was simply ridiculous that he refused to apologize for his past record of homophobic content in his comedy. I am upset by his normalization of scorning the gay community and believe his words absolutely warrant an apology.

At the same time, I recognize that 10 years ago the social and political climate was not the same as it is today; people were generally less accepting of the LGBT community. While this is not

The judgment was long in the making, commencing this summer when West likened slavery to "a choice" and championed conservative pundits Candace Owens and Alex Jones as free thinkers (both have been known to peddle destructive views on politics and race). But in a visit to the *Fader*'s office last week, on the occasion of his forthcoming album *Yandhi*, West paired a rose-red MAGA cap and a sweatshirt with Colin Kaepernick's name inscribed on it—then attempted to broker a meeting between the two poles. "Let's have a dialogue not a diatribe," he tweeted. It's all been a baffling piece of grotesquerie: West celebrates and condemns, enlightens and mocks, preaches peace but fails to practice it. His is a gospel of one—provocation for the sake of performance. (In a group Slack conversation one colleague comically, and accurately, an excuse and does not make the tweets OK, it signifies that they likely did not come from a place of hatred, but of a lack of awareness and education.

Knowing this, I do not see issuing an apology as "feeding the internet trolls." It is recognizing that he has changed and is willing to admit that he was ignorant when he made the homophobic comments. Not only would he be giving an apology that the gay community deserves, but frankly, he would be doing his reputation a favor.

My second problem lies in the typical reaction of an outraged internet looking for another celebrity to "cancel." The act of dragging up a public figure's incriminating old social media posts and declaring them "canceled" is not something only Hart has experienced.

I agree that people should be held accountable for their past actions, no matter if their words were something more acceptable at the time. I also believe that people have the ability to grow as they become more educated. We cannot judge people completely on something they once thought or said.

This online culture of canceling people is toxic behavior.

"The Problem with the Internet's 'Cancel Culture,'" by Calli Masters, Pamplin Media Group, February 7, 2019.

noted of West: "The flat-earthers and hoteps continue to embarrass us any chance they get.")

I found myself among the converts, a former fan turned loud-and-proud dissenter. I once, perhaps ineffectively, argued that West contending with his feelings in the spotlight—as a black man, a husband, a son, a college dropout—was significant in helping to "unsettle this idea of how a black man should act or talk or love when others are watching." In hindsight, I probably could have been less cavalier in my assessment, but I do think he has helped complicate unduly monolithic ideas of public blackness. Only, now I wonder: to what end?

With roots in Black Twitter, cancel culture is an unavoidable mainstay of our infotainment age. In an era of too much everything—TV, opinions, news—we've come to rely on a vocabulary of consolidation: likes, tweets, emoji. Cancel culture is one of these argots—a governor, a self-regulatory device I have come to wield with pride (if infrequent recklessness). In the collective, the gesture is absolute: we can't. We're done. And so we asphyxiate support from a notable cause or figure. Roseanne Barr referred to Valerie Jarrett as an ape? Cancelled. Harvey Weinstein was outed as a sexual predator? Cancelled.

Cancellation is an act of catharsis, of rebellion—and, as such, it has come under fire for being little more than a purity test. Critic Wesley Morris wrapped those arguments into a nifty bow in the *New York Times*: "The conversations are exasperated, the verdicts swift, conclusive and seemingly absolute. The goal is to protect and condemn work, not for its quality, per se, but for its values," he wrote. "The animating crisis of this era is power: the abuse, sharing and stripping of it."

Yes, the cancellation of celebrities, politicians, or sports figures without thought can be a hazardous game. Yet, it's the myth of cancel culture that has earned it such an unsatisfactory veneer. This idea that if, say, Bill Cosby or Logan Paul or Doja Cat was cancelled, it was done so in a rush to judgment. But cancellation does not imply moralism, or heedless impulse—it only requires that we reckon with the truth as it is.

Amid the weeks-long furor, West hasn't entirely been cancelled. He's still afforded a platform, power, a voice. Like Trump, his mutability to the times is both disheartening and damaging, because it serves self-interest under the guise of collective progress. They are cultural barons that spout unity and greatness but go about it with an antagonist's spirit. The more I think about it, the more I'm at peace with divesting from Kanye, a man who hawks empty guru-speak like "Break the simulation" or "We are the solution that heals" as a form of grandstanding.

The frictions of our time are constant and many, and we have no choice but to abate them the best way we can. I've written in the past about my belief that West is a man consumed with search: for identity, for meaning, for genius, always for something more and something eye-opening. But I've come to understand myself in this regard too. Only now, I know not to go searching in the gospel of Kanye West.

> *"Every member of the mainstream and social media mob who falsely attacked, disparaged, or threatened this 16-year-old boy should hang their heads in shame and be held fully accountable in a court of law for their wrongdoing."*

Our Willingness to Jump to Conclusions Is Dangerous

Matthew S. Schwartz

In the following viewpoint, Matthew S. Schwartz reports on the case of a school group that became the target of outrage after a video showing them interacting with a Native American man went viral. Initially, the internet mob went after the students, who appeared in the video to be taunting the man. But an investigation of the incident revealed that looks can be deceiving. The incident illustrates how far things can be taken when internet groups perceive a moral outrage. Matthew S. Schwartz is a reporter for NPR. Previously, he was an award-winning reporter for NPR's WAMO affiliate in Washington, DC.

As you read, consider the following questions:

1. What was the significance of the hats worn by some boys in the high school group in the video?
2. Why were Native American advocates critical of the report exonerating the students?
3. What is the danger of a video such as the one mentioned in this viewpoint going viral?

A private detective agency hired by the diocese that oversees Kentucky's Covington Catholic High School says there's no evidence that the school's students instigated a conflict with a Native American man near the steps of the Lincoln Memorial last month.

The boys, some of whom were wearing red "Make America Great Again" hats, were seen in a video shouting, chanting and grinning at a Native American man, Nathan Phillips. ("Make America great again" was President Trump's campaign slogan.) After the video went viral, the boys faced immediate condemnation from many who said they were intimidating Phillips. Now, a report by independent investigators retained by the Catholic school the boys attend has exonerated the students.

"Our students were placed in a situation that was at once bizarre and even threatening," Diocese of Covington Bishop Roger Foys said in a letter to parents this week. "Their reaction to the situation was, given the circumstances, expected and one might even say laudatory."

The firm hired by the diocese, Greater Cincinnati Investigation, concluded that students made no "offensive or racist statements" to either Phillips or a group of Black Hebrew Israelites and that they didn't perform a "Build the Wall" chant. Investigators said they came to these conclusions after interviewing over 40 students and more than a dozen faculty and parent chaperones, as well as reviewing footage from all major news networks as well as YouTube and Vimeo.

The lawyer for Nick Sandmann, the teenager in the red MAGA hat who responded to Phillips' chanting with an impenetrable smile, condemned the media for rushing to judgment. "Every member of the mainstream and social media mob who falsely attacked, disparaged, or threatened this 16-year-old boy should hang their heads in shame and be held fully accountable in a court of law for their wrongdoing," attorney Lin Wood told the *New York Times*. Wood has said that Phillips will be sued for "lies and false accusations" about Sandmann.

In a statement after the incident, Sandmann said that he didn't feel like he was blocking Phillips' path and that it was "clear" that Phillips "had singled me out for a confrontation." Phillips told NPR that the statement was "a young man trying to alter his story to make himself look good."

Investigators said they tried to interview Phillips at his residence in Ypsilanti, Mich., but over the course of six hours, he never appeared and he has not responded to their request for an interview. "Phillips' public interviews contain some inconsistencies, and we have not been able to resolve them or verify his comments due to our inability to contact him," they said in the report.

Native American advocates were critical of the report. "Maybe they didn't say overtly racist things, but the context of the incident needs to be analyzed," Dina Gilio-Whitaker, professor of American Indian studies at California State University at San Marcos, told the *Washington Post*. She called the report "unfortunate and disgusting" and said it "sidesteps problematic issues—such as the fact they were all wearing MAGA gear, which is, unfortunately, a visual cue."

"We have a history of people in MAGA gear attacking other people," she said.

Investigators said most of the students who wore MAGA hats bought them in Washington, around the time of the March for Life. Some chaperones reported that on past trips, some students had purchased "Hope" hats to support President Barack Obama. In any case, investigators said, the school has no policy banning political apparel on school-sponsored trips.

"The MAGA cap that Nick was wearing provides no legal excuse or justification for the politically motivated accusers," Wood told the *Post*. "Rather, it only confirms their bias and malice."

Investigators found that the kids did perform a "tomahawk chop" to the beat of Phillips' drum and "joined in" with his chanting but said that they could find "no evidence of offensive or racist statements by students to Mr. Phillips or members of his group."

"As far as the tomahawk chop goes," Wood told a pro-life news website, "I am an Atlanta Braves fan and the tomahawk chop is a fan cheer at baseball games that is intended to support the team and is not intended to disparage Native Americans."

The person who said on video that "it's not rape if you enjoy it" was not a student at Covington Catholic, the investigators also found.

Before the investigation, the diocese had said the boys could be expelled for their behavior. In his letter to parents, Bishop Roy said he was pleased that his "hope and expectation" that the boys would be exonerated "has been realized." The students, who had traveled to Washington to "march peacefully" for the anti-abortion rally, "could never have expected what they experienced on the steps of the Lincoln Memorial while waiting for the buses to take them home," Roy wrote. "Their stance there was surely a pro-life stance. I commend them."

> *"As political affiliation becomes more and more a matter of tribal identity, patrolling the borders of the in-group and singling out enemies takes on increasing importance."*

Cancel Culture Is Itself One of Society's Problems

Sarah Ditum

In the following viewpoint, Sarah Ditum argues that cancel culture has become its own societal problem. The author describes the phenomenon almost as one would describe the scourge of drugs on society. There is a "high" in calling out people, but ultimately the effects of the actions don't do much except for possibly ruining someone's life. It is troubling, she writes, that society has adopted shunning as a method of activism. Sarah Ditum is a freelance writer on politics, culture and lifestyle who writes regularly for the Guardian, New Statesman, *and other publications.*

As you read, consider the following questions:

1. Why does the author open with the statement that cancel culture has been canceled by Barack Obama?
2. How does the viewpoint define cancellation?
3. How do the left and right view cancel culture differently, according to the viewpoint?

Cancel culture has been cancelled by Barack Obama. Rejoice! Now a long-established ritual of social media, to be "cancelled" or "called out" means to be subject to severe public contempt on account of some infraction against morality.

It can spill into lost jobs, broken friendships and public protests; ultimately, it amounts to an effort to declare the victim a non-person, someone intolerable to decent society. No appeals and no rehabilitation.

Speaking last week at the Obama Foundation summit, the former president told his audience: "This idea of purity and you're never compromised and you're always politically 'woke' and all that stuff. You should get over that quickly."

There was a tendency, he said, for the politically engaged—and he was particularly addressing those on the left—to trade in comforting simplicity and the dehumanisation of opponents. His comments hold a lot of gratifying truths, but the most important one is this: cancelling people feels great. "Like, if I tweet or hashtag about how you didn't do something right or used the wrong verb, then I can sit back and feel pretty good about myself," he said. "Cause, 'Man, you see how woke I was, I called you out.'"

For those doing the cancelling, it's a righteous high, a buzz of benediction, a most holy moment of delight. Because when it comes to the call-out, we can all tell ourselves we're doing it for the best of reasons.

We want to build a better world. We want to help our fellow citizens correct their error and protect the vulnerable from harm. And how could there be anything mean or shabby about that?

What a load of self-aggrandising bunk. Cancellation is an intoxicating blend of piousness plus power. The online pile-on is a kind of wild justice and participating in its scourging force is a tremendous thrill. Even better if you have the nous to harness and direct that outrage for yourself. The Twitterverse is studded with micro-celebrities of affront who have raised themselves to prominence on a tide of other people's anger.

If you have a particularly morbid fascination with this stuff, you can watch a portrait of one of them in the documentary *Who Is Arthur Chu?* (available on Amazon Prime). Chu leveraged a successful run on the US gameshow *Jeopardy!* into a respectable Twitter following, then segued into leftwing activism, targeting individuals he deems harmful; now, he commands several thousand dollars a time for delivering talks on subjects such as "toxic masculinity."

Chu claims to be motivated by anger against injustice. But when, in an unguarded moment on camera, he talks about what success means to him, he doesn't refer to policy or social change: he talks about how he has nearly doubled his number of followers.

Inevitably, given that he's a beneficiary of the cancel culture, Chu is one of the most adamant when it comes to asserting that cancel culture is not actually a problem. For its leftwing defenders, the label is a politicised tag designed to delegitimise rightful critique. A widely circulated image from the webcomic XKCD sums up the position. "If you're yelled at, boycotted, have your show cancelled, or get banned from an internet community, your free speech rights aren't being violated," says the stick figure presenting the voice of reason. "It's just that the people listening think you're an a**hole and they're showing you the door."

This is one of those arguments that's true as far as it goes, but doesn't go very far. What if there were an argument against yelling/boycotting/cancelling/banning that didn't consist solely of claims to freedom of speech? (Obama doesn't refer to free speech at all in his comments, talking instead about the power of conversation to change minds.)

Another defence is to point to the ostracism of unarguably despicable figures as evidence that cancel culture is actually a good thing—a *Washington Post* op-ed last week cited the calling out of Harvey Weinstein at a recent public event and argued that "critics of 'cancel culture' really just hate democracy."

Well, maybe. But it's possible to both approve the shunning of a man subject to widely accepted accusations of sexual assault and also worry about the adoption of shunning as a universal tool of activism.

Meanwhile, on the right, there's a comfortable certainty that cancel culture is a strictly leftish vice.

The rightwing commentator Douglas Murray, invited on to BBC Radio 4's *Today* programme to discuss Obama's comments, described the quest for "wrongthink" as the purview of his ideological opponents. But it won't be the left squirming in moral horror when someone dares to show up on the BBC sans poppy between now and Armistice Day. (Bonus: Murray got to play the cancel culture victim when the host Nick Robinson challenged him on his past remarks.)

So the right has its cancel culture and pretends to abhor it; the left, less hypocritically but more incoherently, digs in to defend the indefensible.

Obama is, of course, correct. The pursuit of purity is not just a wound in civil society, it's also the opposite of politics. "That's not activism. That's not bringing about change," he said. "If all you're doing is casting stones, you're probably not going to get that far." But he assumes here that people engage in politics in order to bring about change and I'm not sure that's true.

As political affiliation becomes more and more a matter of tribal identity, patrolling the borders of the in-group and singling out enemies takes on increasing importance. After all, it just feels good.

> *"The traditional great man theory, which centres on the driving creative genius of individual—usually white—men, has been challenged. As a result, it has transformed our understanding of how knowledge and art are produced."*

Cancellation Reveals a Lack of Examination of How We Understand Culture

Tina Sikka

In the following viewpoint, Tina Sikka argues that canceling figures in art and culture fails to take into account the involvement of others in the creation of their art. This is because great artistic and cultural achievements have historically been attributed to men as if they'd done the work alone. In truth, the author argues, there were frequently wives, assistants, or teams behind the man. If we decide to stop watching a popular TV show because of one problematic star, then we are discounting the contributions of the other actors, writers, producers, and crew. Tina Sikka is a lecturer in media and culture studies at Newcastle University and the author of The Ethics of GeoEngineering: Climate Change and Feminist Empiricism.

"Two Arguments to Help Decide Whether to 'Cancel' Someone and Their Work," by Tina Sikka, The Conversation, December 12, 2019. https://theconversation.com/two-arguments-to-help-decide-whether-to-cancel-someone-and-their-work-128411. Licensed under CC BY-ND 4.0.

As you read, consider the following questions:

1. What is the great man theory, according to the viewpoint?
2. What is the death of the author theory?
3. Which theory does the author endorse?

While definitions vary, to "cancel" in today's lingo means to remove people and cultural products from consumption and popular conversation. This is done in light of actions that make them unworthy of praise or critique.

Notable cancellations include R. Kelly over allegations of sexual abuse, Gwen Stefani for apparent cultural appropriation in the 1990s and early 2000s, Roseanne Barr for a racist tweet, and Kanye West for being a Trump supporter. There are a myriad of things that can lead to an individual, and by proxy their work, being cancelled.

At present, there exists a lack of critical examination of how we treat art and culture by people who have been cancelled. We tend to understand culture from the view of "Great Man theory," which argues that the genius and ingenuity of one person (typically a man) was responsible for the creation of a thing. It is largely mocked now as we better understand the nature of the village around a creator and marginalised individuals receive acknowledgement posthumously.

It also relies on the neglect of what should be a natural fit for progressive politics—an embrace of the "death of the author." Asserted first by Roland Barthes in 1967, it became iconic in literary theory and later film and cultural analysis. It argues that, culturally, we live in a time in which it is the audience, not the author, who has ultimate control over the interpretation of arts and culture.

Not the Work of One

There is a lot of recent writing reflecting on the role women (particularly wives and partners), people of colour and low-paid assistants played in the making of artistic, scientific and cultural

Sh**posting

Sh**posting is posting "aggressively, ironically, and of trollishly poor quality" posts or content to an online forum or social network. Sh**posts are intentionally designed to derail discussions or cause the biggest reaction with the least amount of effort possible. Sometimes they are made as part of a coordinated flame war to make the site unusable to its regular visitors

Sh**posting is a modern form of provocation on the internet, but the concept is not new. Early 20th century art movements such as Dadaism or Surrealism created art that was intentionally low quality or offensive to provoke the art world.

Writing in *Polygon*, Sam Greszes compared sh**posting to Dadaism's "confusing, context-free pieces that, specifically because they were so absurd, were seen as revolutionary works both artistically and politically." Greszes writes that the goal of sh**posting is "to make an audience so confused at the lack of content that they laugh or smile."

The political uses of sh**posting came to prominence during the 2016 United States presidential election. In May of that year, the *Daily Dot* wrote that a sh**post is "a deliberate provocation designed for maximum impact with minimum effort."

works. This has been seen in the case of the discovery of DNA, contributions to chemistry and the invention of the light bulb.

As such, the traditional great man theory, which centres on the driving creative genius of individual—usually white—men, has been challenged. As a result, it has transformed our understanding of how knowledge and art are produced.

Even iconic works of art that lean into the great man trope have subsequently been found to be based on faulty assumptions. Michelangelo, for example, who was more familiar with sculpture than painting, on receiving the commission of the Sistine Chapel, recruited a number of assistants who worked directly on the ceiling fresco.

In September 2016, the pro-Trump group Nimble America received widespread media attention. The *Daily Beast* described the group as "dedicated to 'sh**posting' and circulating internet memes maligning Hillary Clinton."

In September 2016, the *Independent* wrote that sh**posting is an apolitical "tool that can be put to a variety of effects." However, posts such as these appeared long before the 2016 US presidential election.

In November 2016, *Esquire* magazine wrote that "internet mockery was emerging as a legitimate political technique: sh**posting. Maybe the 2020 election would be all sh**posting."

In March 2018, talking about Facebook group New Urbanist Sh**posting or New Urbanist Memes for Transit-Oriented Teens, *Chicago* magazine defined it as "posts that are meant to be awkward and irrelevant, aggravating and distracting social media communities from discussing their topic at hand."

In 2019, the BBC's political editor Laura Kuenssberg incorrectly described sh**posting as "political parties or campaign groups make an advert that looks really rubbish and people share it online saying, 'Oh I can't believe how sh** this is' then it gets shared and shared and shared and shared and they go, 'Ha, job done.'"

"Sh**posting," wikipedia.org

In film and television there is a complicated division of labour among all the players, in front of and behind the camera, who have a vital role in getting something produced. To identify and apportion acclaim or blame to one person, however terrible they are as individuals, simultaneously penalises everyone else involved in the production process.

This was seen in the case of Roseanne Barr whose tweet led to the rest of the cast and crew losing their jobs as *Roseanne* was taken off air. This is an example of how great man theory, in a contemporary context, can be extended to women who are now in positions of power where their social infractions can lead to the punishment of the other producers of their work.

This approach perpetuates the individualistic (rather than social), mostly male genius-driven model of history and innovation. Ironically, this is the case even when we evaluate culture from a place of critique and warranted derision. As such, perhaps it might be worth considering whether or not to consume a piece of culture with which a cancelled individual has been involved, with this perspective in mind.

The Audience Is in Control

Also worth considering is the "death of the author" theory. This perspective has been made famous by the rise of postmodernism— defined briefly as a reaction against modernity's trust in hard and fast truths and faith in progress, as well as an artistic push to rebel against cultural conventions.

Essentially, what Barthes argues is that cultural works do not have a singular, secret meaning that we must look for. Rather, it is a revolutionary act to use our own power of interpretation to read things differently. The application of this idea has produced illuminating and transgressive readings of culture and art. This includes feminist readings of films that are misogynistic when viewed superficially, but which can also be read as exposing the fragility of dominant masculinity when examined using a feminist lens.

A good example of this can be found in an essay by the writer Zaron Burnett III in which he makes a persuasive case for reading Disney's *The Little Mermaid* as a feminist text. For instance, in the song "Part of Your World," in which Ariel articulates her desire to challenge social norms and gain agency.

How we might harness this in the context of work marred by cancelled individuals ranges from ignoring their involvement entirely to embracing personal interpretations based on our individual life experiences.

Yet the way in which cancel culture handles such works seems to have swung violently in the opposite direction, resulting in the death of the audience and, in particular, of audience agency. People are not afforded the space to form such personal readings. Instead, a singular narrative prevails that gives no room for any other action than to cancel. Some examples include ongoing arguments in favour of cancelling the art of Paul Gauguin, refusing to watch or screen films involving Roman Polanski, and the network cancellations of *Cosby Show* reruns.

Taken together, the "great man" and "death of the author" frameworks should, at the very least, provide further food for thought. While it is inevitably up to the consumer of culture to decide where they stand and what they feel comfortable consuming, it is worthwhile to consider unorthodox perspectives. Ultimately, isn't that precisely what great art should challenge you to do?

> *"If you feel self-conscious about what*
> *you say and write now, imagine what*
> *it was like in East Germany: when*
> *one in 30 of your fellow citizens is*
> *an informer looking out for a reason*
> *to 'call you out' to the secret police;*
> *when being 'canceled' for saying the*
> *wrong thing could get you arrested*
> *and worse."*

Cancel Culture Is a Reminder That We Still Enjoy Freedom of Speech

Dan Sanchez

In the following viewpoint, Dan Sanchez argues that there is no doubt that "wokeness" is promoting a cancel-happy culture in which people are afraid to express themselves for fear of saying the wrong thing and putting their livelihoods at risk. However, the author contends, rarely are the consequences for saying the wrong thing as dramatic as they would be if Americans did not enjoy freedom of speech. In its own way, he says, cancel culture is evidence of our freedoms. Dan Sanchez is the director of content at the Foundation for Economic Education (FEE) and the editor-in chief of FEE.org.

As you read, consider the following questions:

1. What type of public figures does the viewpoint discuss in its opening and why did the author choose them?
2. Why isn't criticizing enough for many activists, according to the viewpoint?
3. What is China encouraging its university students to do?

YouTube stars Jeffree Star and Shane Dawson have joined forces to release a makeup line called the Conspiracy Collection. In a mere 30 minutes, the duo sold one million palettes of eyeshadow. The demand was so huge, it crashed Shopify for several hours.

Star and Dawson seem to be riding high, which is especially remarkable since they have both gone through potentially career-ending controversies. Star has been caught on video using racist language, and Dawson has been accused of cruelty to animals.

YouTube celebs get caught up in scandals a lot. PewDiePie, Logan Paul, Philip De Franco, and many more have run the internet's gauntlet of shame. Whether you've double-crossed a friend a la James Charles and Tati Westbrook, or you've ripped off your fans a la TanaCon, the cancel cops will find you.

Obama vs. Call-Out Culture

And it goes way beyond YouTube. Cancel culture has taken root in almost every public arena, from show business to academia. It has even seeped into private life. Do you ever feel super-self-conscious whenever conversation touches upon a sensitive subject? Like you're walking on eggshells? Like a single mistake in word choice will cause offense or draw condemnation? Then you've experienced wokeness run amok.

For many activists, criticism isn't enough. There must be real consequences. And the biggest prize is the target's livelihood: to get them fired, deplatformed, or otherwise canceled.

In a sense, cancel culture is nothing new, and is actually essential. All communities need norms. And an essential way to enforce norms has always been to denounce ("call out") norm-breakers, or even to ostracize ("cancel") them in extreme cases. Some of the YouTubers mentioned above deserved to be called out for what they said or did.

But it can go too far. Cancel culture becomes oppression when it descends into fanaticism, paranoia, and censorship.

And there does seem to be a growing weariness with wokeness. Dave Chapelle pushed back hard against cancel culture in his Netflix special *Sticks and Stones*. He caught flak for it, but he has also since been awarded the Mark Twain Prize for American Humor.

And Barack Obama recently called out call-out culture, when he said:

> I do get a sense sometimes now among certain young people, and this is accelerated by social media, there is this sense sometimes of: "The way of me making change is to be as judgmental as possible about other people, and that's enough." Like, if I tweet or hashtag about how you didn't do something right or used the wrong verb, then I can sit back and feel pretty good about myself because "man, you see how woke I was. I called you out." (…) That's not activism. That's not bringing about change.

One thing worth appreciating is that our cancel culture could be a lot worse. After all, none of the YouTubers listed above have been canceled permanently. They've been chastised. Some have apologized. Some have changed their ways. But they all bounced back. They all still have millions of fans, and many have millions of dollars, too.

If you're one of those fans—if you get a lot of entertainment, value, or even inspiration from any of them—you might especially appreciate the fact that, in spite of their imperfections, your favorite YouTuber can still put out content and merch.

And you know what we have to thank for that? Freedom of speech.

Canceled by the State

Freedom of speech has faded in popularity lately. Many see it as an unjust defense of hate speech and political lies. But "call-out/cancel culture" would be much worse without it.

When the government can decide what is unacceptable speech and can enforce that decision with physical violence, calling someone out, or getting them canceled, takes on a whole new meaning.

China doesn't have freedom of speech, and this has many ramifications for its people. For example, the government of China is encouraging university students to report (call out) their professors for expressions of dissent. Such reports have resulted in many professors being fired or suspended (canceled). The *New York Times* recently interviewed one of many student informers in China:

> With a neon-red backpack and white Adidas shoes, he looks like any other undergraduate on the campus of Sichuan University in southwestern China.
>
> But Peng Wei, a 21-year-old chemistry major, has a special mission: He is both student and spy.
>
> Mr. Peng is one of a growing number of "student information officers" who keep tabs on their professors' ideological views. They are there to help root out teachers who show any sign of disloyalty to President Xi Jinping and the ruling Communist Party.
>
> "It's our duty to make sure that the learning environment is pure," Mr. Peng said, "and that professors are following the rules."

This is a throwback to China's Cultural Revolution of the 1960s and 70s, when the government of Mao Zedong encouraged students to not only inform on their teachers, but to ritually humiliate any who were not ideologically pure.

How about canceling YouTubers? The Chinese government has canceled all of YouTube for China's entire population of 1.4 billion. China also has a habit of "canceling" foreign creators and media over messages it disapproves of.

Free speech was also absent in communist East Germany. Like China, the East German secret police (the Stasi) encouraged ordinary citizens to become informers: to call out their neighbors, friends, even family for any speech that betrayed ideological impurity or disloyalty. This created what has been called "a culture of denunciation." The East German government weaponized "call-out culture" against its own people. As Wendy McElroy wrote:

> The Stasi had eyes and ears everywhere, so that people did not speak in the streets; they whispered in their own homes and were wary of speaking freely to family or friends. To contradict the state was treason, for which a person could be imprisoned and tortured in order to produce more names. Sometimes people were executed.

McElroy quotes historian David Cook:

> During the lifespan of the communist regime in East Germany [1949–1990] it is estimated from existing archival material that there were up to 500,000 informers active at various times. Or more starkly one in 30 of the population had worked for the Stasi by the fall of the GDR.

If you feel self-conscious about what you say and write now, imagine what it was like in East Germany: when one in 30 of your fellow citizens is an informer looking out for a reason to "call you out" to the secret police; when being "canceled" for saying the wrong thing could get you arrested and worse.

Imagine how boring YouTube would be under oppression like that, if it was allowed to exist at all.

Without freedom of speech, once the government decides you're canceled: end of story. But in a free society, even if you're called out or canceled by an internet outrage mob, there's room for debate, apologies, pushback, forgiveness, learning, and growth on all sides. See, for example, these YouTuber tweets.

James Charles *@james Charles*

I made my video today NOT to start a war, but to take responsibility for my actions & clear my name. There ARE two sides to every story, & now you've heard both. I'm sure more will be said, but I'm moving on. You can form your opinions, but PLEASE do not send any hate to anyone.

3:18 PM May 18, 2019

tana mongeau *@tanamongeau*

i love u @shanedawson... like family. i know where your hearts at & what you would and wouldn't do. seeing how much you've grown from your past is the biggest inspiration to me. here's to every 6 months when they wanna cancel u for JOKES you've APOLOGIZED for & grown from.

9:42 PM Mar 18, 2019

Freedom of speech is messy, but it works and we need it. Don't give it up.

Periodical and Internet Sources Bibliography

The following articles have been selected to supplement the diverse views presented in this chapter.

Katie Camero, "What Is 'Cancel Culture'? J. K. Rowling Controversy Leaves Writers, Scholars Debating," *Miami Herald*, July 8, 2020. https://www.miamiherald.com/news/nation-world/national /article244082037.html

Cassie Da Costa, "Harvey Weinstein's Actors Hour Fiasco and the Illusion of 'Cancel Culture,'" *Daily Beast*, October 30, 2019. https://www.thedailybeast.com/harvey-weinsteins-actors-hour -fiasco-and-the-illusion-of-cancel-culture

Ross Douthat, "10 Theses About Cancel Culture," *New York Times*, July 14, 2020. https://www.nytimes.com/2020/07/14/opinion /cancel-culture-.html

Susannah Goldsbrough, "Cancel Culture: What It Is, and How Did It Begin?" Telegraph.com, July 30, 2020. https://www.telegraph .co.uk/music/what-to-listen-to/cancel-culture-did-begin/

Sarah Hagi, "Cancel Culture Is Not Real—At Least Not in the Way People Think," *Time*, November 21, 2019. https://time .com/5735403/cancel-culture-is-not-real/

Harper's Magazine, "A Letter on Justice and Open Debate," July 7, 2020. https://harpers.org/a-letter-on-justice-and-open-debate/

Daphne Keller, "Facebook Restricts Speech by Popular Demand," *Atlantic*, September 22, 2019. https://www.theatlantic.com /ideas/archive/2019/09/facebook-restricts-free-speech-popular -demand/598462/

Danielle Kurtzleben, "When Republicans Attack 'Cancel Culture,' What Does It Mean?" NPR, February 10, 2021. https://www.npr. org/2021/02/10/965815679/is-cancel-culture-the-future-of-the- gop

Helen Lewis, "How Capitalism Drives Cancel Culture," *Atlantic*, July 14, 2020. https://www.theatlantic.com/international

/archive/2020/07/cancel-culture-and-problem-woke
-capitalism/614086/

Ryan Lizza, "Americans Tune In to 'Cancel Culture'—And Don't Like What They See," *Politico*, July 22, 2020. https://www.politico.com /news/2020/07/22/americans-cancel-culture-377412

Dora Mekovar, "Is Cancel Culture Killing Free Exchange of Ideas?" Voice of America, August 11, 2020. https://www.voanews.com /usa/all-about-america/cancel-culture-killing-free-exchange-ideas

Ligaya Mishan, "The Long and Tortured History of Cancel Culture," *New York Times*, December 3, 2020. https://www.nytimes .com/2020/12/03/t-magazine/cancel-culture-history.html

CHAPTER 4

| Will Cancel Culture
Be Canceled?

Chapter Preface

Cancel culture is actually nothing new to human societies. As journalist Joel Stein wrote in *LA Magazine*:

> Cancel culture sprung up out of nowhere approximately 50,000 years ago. Exiling tribe members who violated a core value was an effective, if pretty cruel, way to convince everyone in the tribe not to show up late for battles …
>
> Like everything, banishment falls in and out of fashion. It heats up when society changes its norms because ostracism is a great marketing gimmick. Sure, banishment is blunt, inelegant, and does little to change opinions, but that's not the point. The point is to scare the tribe into adjusting its behavior.

But of course, there is something new about cancel culture, and that is the technology used to carry it out. Today's cancel culture is a digital version of a vigilante mob.

Maybe the most important and impactful difference is how effective technology is in calling out someone or something—how easily and how quickly technology has made public cancelings and humiliations commonplace, with retributions made fierce and swift.

In his article on cancel culture, published on the website New Discourses, Roy Meredith contends that cancel culture is not a product of liberalism or of truly liberal societies, nor is it real justice for oppressed groups. Rather, it is the creation of a pseudo scholarship called Critical Social Justice, which flattens and simplifies everything into a pursuit of power, using the tactics of mobs and a totalitarian ideology.

Cancel culture is unlikely to be a trend or a phase or to go away on its own, though it might take different forms as technology and society evolve. Which is why respectful, open discussion and thoughtful criticism should be encouraged.

> "Content that sparks an intense
> emotional response—positive or
> negative—is more likely to go viral.
> … Outrage is the perfect negative
> emotion to attract attention and
> engagement—and algorithms are
> primed to pounce."

Algorithms Are to Blame for Today's Cancel Culture

Anjana Susaria

In the following viewpoint, Anjana Susaria argues that the conditions for the proliferation of cancel culture are in part due to technology, particularly social media. Social media is driven by algorithms, and it thrives on emotional responses such as outrage, making it the perfect delivery system for being canceled. However, those same algorithms that can bring a person down can also build them back up. Anjana Susaria is associate professor of information systems at Michigan State University.

"Hate Cancel Culture? Blame Algorithms," by Anjana Susaria, The Conversation, January 28, 2020. https://theconversation.com/hate-cancel-culture-blame-algorithms-129402. Licensed under CC BY-ND 4.0.

As you read, consider the following questions:

1. According to the viewpoint, how do algorithms work?
2. How did cancel culture affect comedian Kevin Hart?
3. How can cancel culture be good for business, according to the author?

"Cancel culture" has become so pervasive that even former President Barack Obama has weighed in on the phenomenon, describing it as an overly judgmental approach to activism that does little to bring about change.

For the uninitiated, here's a quick primer on the phenomenon: An individual or an organization says, supports or promotes something that other people find offensive. They swarm, piling on the criticism via social media channels. Then that person or company is largely shunned, or "canceled."

It happened to Chick-fil-A when its ties to organizations such as Focus on the Family invited backlash from LGBTQ activists; it happened to YouTube influencer James Charles, who was accused of betraying his former mentor and lost millions of followers; and it happened to Miami Dolphins owner Stephen Ross after people learned he had held a fundraiser for President Trump.

Outrage can spread so quickly on social media that companies or individuals who don't adequately respond to a mishap—intentional or not—can face swift backlash. You can send a thoughtless tweet before boarding a flight and, upon landing, realize you've become the target of global ire.

A lot of attention has been given to repercussions of cancel culture on celebrities, from JK Rowling, to Kevin Hart to Lena Dunham.

Less talked about is the way algorithms actually perpetuate cancel culture.

Algorithms Love Outrage

My own research has shown how content that sparks an intense emotional response—positive or negative—is more likely to go viral.

Out of millions of tweets, posts, videos and articles, social media users can be exposed to only a handful. So platforms write algorithms that curate news feeds to maximize engagement; social media companies, after all, want you to spend as much time on their platforms as possible.

Outrage is the perfect negative emotion to attract attention and engagement—and algorithms are primed to pounce. One person tweeting her outrage would normally fall largely on deaf ears. But if that one person is able to attract enough initial engagement, algorithms will extend that individual's reach by promoting it to like-minded individuals. A snowball effect occurs, creating a feedback loop that amplifies the outrage.

Often, this outrage can lack context or be misleading. But that can work in its favor. In fact, I've found that misleading content on social media tends to lead to even more engagement than verified information.

So you can write an immature tweet as a teenager, someone can dig it up, express outrage, conveniently leave out that it's from seven or eight years ago, and the algorithms will nonetheless amplify the reaction.

All of a sudden, you're canceled.

Hart Goes Down

We saw this dynamic recently play out with actor Kevin Hart.

Once it was announced that Hart would be the host for the 2019 Academy Awards, Twitter users plumbed a series of homophobic tweets from 2009 to 2011 and started sharing them. Few were aware Hart had tweeted about homosexuality. The outrage was swift.

Hart's unapologetic response on Instagram inflamed the online anger.

Algorithms anticipate what users want based on detailed information about their preferences. All of a sudden, those most likely to be upset by Hart's homophobic remarks were having tweets about them splashed across their feeds.

Within a day of Hart's Instagram post, the actor announced he would withdraw from hosting.

Cancel culture is just one outgrowth of social media algorithms.

More broadly, people have criticized how algorithms such as YouTube's actively promote divisive posts in order to suck people into spending more time online.

In 2018, a British Parliament committee report on fake news criticized Facebook's "relentless targeting of hyper-partisan views, which play to the fears and prejudices of people."

Algorithms Encourage Second Acts

Paradoxically, the same algorithmic forces that buttress cancel culture can actually rehabilitate canceled entertainers.

A few months after the Hart controversy, Netflix decided to produce two shows featuring the comedian.

Why would Netflix expose itself to criticism by elevating a supposedly canceled celebrity?

Because it knew that there would be an audience for Hart's comedy—that, in certain circles, the fact that he had been canceled made him that much more appealing.

Like social media platforms, Netflix also deploys algorithms. Because Netflix has a massive library of content, it deploys algorithms that take into account users' prior viewing choices and preferences to recommend specific shows and movies.

Maybe these users are die-hard Hart fans. Or maybe they're inclined see Hart as a victim of political correctness. Either way, Netflix has granular data about which users would be predisposed to watching a show about Hart, despite the fact that he had been nominally canceled.

On Netflix's end, there's little risk. Netflix probably knows, on some level, which of its subscribers are likely to be offended by

Hart. So it simply won't promote Hart's show to those people. At the same time, partnering with controversial brands and individuals can be good for business.

Together, the phenomenon of cancel culture is an illustration of the weird ways algorithms and social media can upend, distort and rehabilitate the lives and careers of celebrities.

> *"There is a term for older people who benefitted from the boom and are now criticising young people for wanting change too quickly, and I think it's: OK, boomer."*

We've Reached the Point Where We Are Canceling an Entire Generation

Poppy Noor

In the following viewpoint, Poppy Noor illustrates a trend in cancel culture by criticizing—perhaps tongue in cheek—former president Barack Obama's centrist, generally popular opinions with the dismissive phrase, "OK Boomer." This condescending phrase, with its reference to the aging Baby Boom generation, is intended to immediately shut down commentary deigned by those who think they are in the know as out of touch and un-woke. The author takes issue with Obama's criticisms of cancel culture, but her desire to cancel Obama with the response "OK Boomer" plays right into Obama's point. Poppy Noor is a feature writer for the Guardian *and a contributor to* Vice.

As you read, consider the following questions:

1. How did Barack Obama criticize the Black Lives Matter movement?
2. What does the author think about Obama's stance on radical change?
3. Why does the viewpoint mention Bernie Sanders?

Barack Obama took to the stage at an event in Singapore on Monday to ponder one the world's most revolutionary questions: wouldn't the world be better if it were run by women?

He said: "Now, women, I just want you to know: you are not perfect, but what I can say pretty indisputably is that you're better than us [men]."

Some have questioned Obama's motives: is he just taking a shot at Bernie Sanders? Others called him condescending, equating his statement to the men who praise their stay-at-home wives for doing "the most important job in the world."

Would it be uncouth to say that Obama has become … a centrist dad? Who lectures people with extremely mundane, unsolicited opinions?

Here are some past examples:

1. When He Told Black Lives Matter to Stop Yelling

In 2016, Obama met young people in Europe and was asked whether his administration had gone far enough in tackling racial profiling. Instead of answering the question, Obama turned his attention towards the Black Lives Matter movement.

"Once you've highlighted an issue and brought it to people's attention … then you can't just keep on yelling at them," Obama said.

And so, the president who ran on a campaign promising people "Yes, we can" was using his platform to criticize a campaign group working to highlight how routinely American police shoot and kill unarmed black men.

2. When He Complained About Woke Culture

When Obama took the stage to talk down to young people in October, it was almost too easy to agree with him. The world is messy, he said, so we should be more careful about our tendency to "cancel" people online—especially if our judgment is replacing real action.

Which all sounds fair enough. But then came his central message: that change is incremental. "We can't completely remake society in a minute. This idea of purity and you're never compromised and you're always politically woke … you should get over that quickly," he said.

There is a term for older people who benefitted from the boom and are now criticising young people for wanting change too quickly, and I think it's: OK, boomer.

3. When He Said America Was Not Ready for Real Change

In November, Obama—who now has a net worth of $70m—stood up in front of a room of similarly wealthy people to reassure them that the system doesn't need to be radically changed.

"Even as we push the envelope and we are bold in our vision, we also have to be rooted in reality," Obama said at the annual Democracy Alliance meeting, attended by wealthy liberal donors. "The average American doesn't think we have to completely tear down the system and remake it."

Perhaps Americans wanting radical change should re-think their approach. Get ready to lean in to good health insurance, everybody!

4. When He Bragged About Helping Oil Companies

At a Rice University gala in 2018, Obama took credit for the oil and gas boom in America. "It went up every year I was president. Suddenly America's the biggest oil producer and the biggest gas. That was me, people, say thank you," he said.

Oil production grew 88% under Obama's two terms. The US is also one of the biggest consumers of fossil fuels, and the planet is literally burning—so this is not exactly something to be proud of, but credit where credit is due, I guess.

5. When He Said He'd Stand Up to Stop Sanders

Obama has said he would support any Democratic nominee for president in 2020. But judging by a Politico report from November, he doesn't include Bernie Sanders in that list. The piece quoted close sources to him who said that Obama has refrained from speaking out against Bernie so far because Sanders doesn't look like a credible threat.

But privately, Politico reported, Obama has vowed to "speak up to stop him" if it looks like Sanders has a proper shot at winning the nomination.

"That cancel culture may simply be brushing aside those individuals who don't fit into a collective vision of the future is troubling, and may actually be serving as a direct antithesis to the mission of social justice at the end of the day."

Cancel Culture Is a Band-Aid Solution

Quentin Thomas

In the following viewpoint, Quentin Thomas argues that the swift "justice" inherent in call-out culture does not allow for the canceled person to learn and grow from their mistake. The author compares cancel culture to our prison system, in that prison offers punishment without the rehabilitation necessary to avoid recidivism. Similarly, cancel culture is swift to punish but fails to hold people accountable for their irresponsibilities. Quentin Thomas is an opinion writer for the Brown Daily Herald *and is the vice president of Brown University's NAACP chapter.*

"Thomas '21: Cancelling Cancel Culture," by Quentin Thomas, The *Brown Daily Herald*, November 6, 2018. Reprinted by permission.

As you read, consider the following questions:

1. Is canceling a tool for social justice, according to the viewpoint?
2. Why did canceling Roseanne Barr fall short, according to the author?
3. How does the viewpoint relate cancel culture to the prison industrial complex?

The practice of "cancelling" is becoming increasingly common. By cancelling, I mean the process by which people mark someone as problematic and withdraw any and all prior support to ignore and exclude this person. To a lesser degree, when I talk about "cancel culture" I'm also referring to the broader habit our society has of simply doing away with those it finds undesirable. One way this manifests is when celebrities' old, problematic tweets resurface and people decide to cancel them in retaliation. It is important to remember that actions do have consequences, and folks absolutely should be held accountable for disrespectful or mean-spirited behavior. However, we should also think about

CANCEL CULTURE IS TOXIC

2019 brought into focus the "cancel culture" (named Macquarie Dictionary's Word of the Year 2019). Cancel culture is toxic, it's a term that captures an important aspect of the past year's Zeitgeist. It's an attitude which is so pervasive that it now has a name. Cancel culture has become, for better or worse, a powerful force, according to the said dictionary's committee.

Cancel culture refers to mass social media boycotting of celebrities (or regular folks) for violating rules in the past that may not even have been obvious at the time. It is a modern internet phenomenon. It is commonly caused by an accusation, whether that accusation has merit or not. Basically, the ones boycotting the person are quick to judge and slow to question.

what it means for us to immediately close someone off. I believe it's worth thinking about what accountability looks like beyond simply exiling someone. In doing so, we can position ourselves more firmly within the values of social justice.

One reason worth giving cancel culture a hard examination is that it doesn't seem to be working. If cancel culture is meant to be a tool for social justice, cancelling people and not paying them any mind would compel them to look at their actions and take the time to understand why what they've done or said might not be in good taste. While the idea of cancelling someone might be well-intentioned and intended to inspire some introspection and critical thought on the part of the individual being cancelled, rarely does this learning manifest on its own. For example, this past summer Roseanne Barr had the reboot of her show cancelled by ABC following a racist tweet she made about Valerie Jarrett, a former adviser to former president Barack Obama. As a result, Barr was forced to apologize in hopes of reacquiring a spot in the public's good graces.

However, in her apologies to Jarrett, it was clear that Barr had not really grasped an understanding of why she had warranted

Comedian Sarah Silverman was fired from a movie she was cast in recently, after a 2007 photo of her in blackface resurfaced. She has already apologized for the photo, going so far as to draw attention to it in a magazine interview. Silverman argued on the Bill Simmons podcast that cancel culture leaves no room for growth. Additionally, she said that social shaming is "really scary."

When two allegations of sexual misconduct against Katy Perry were reported, there was a campaign on Twitter to cancel the singer. Search the hashtags #KatyPerryIsOverParty or #SurvivingKatyPerry, a play on the "Surviving R. Kelly" documentary that exposed R Kelly's history of sexual assault.

"Cancel Culture Is Toxic, What to Expect in 2020," by Kasmin Fernandes, The *CSR Journal*, January 6, 2020.

criticism. Further, her apology doesn't show her raising her critical consciousness or being more mindful with her language. In other words, nowhere in her apology did Barr say that this fiasco prompted a change in her politics, a hard look in the mirror, an interrogation of the ways in which she perpetuated racism or a lifelong commitment to unlearning racial privilege on her part. This is not to question the validity of Barr's facing consequences for her actions. Rather, I'm arguing that effectively shutting Barr out might provide an immediate band-aid solution to the problem, but it also provides no real impetus for Barr to critically examine and think about why, exactly, her tweet was problematic, why she was criticized and why her show was cancelled.

Recognizing that cancel culture is not resulting in the learning and changed behavior of cancelled individuals is precisely why I propose a shift in how we deal with people who have said or done irresponsible things. Thinking through what it means to hold people accountable is more in line with the social justice ideals that cancel culture is—at its most basic level—rooted in. That cancel culture may simply be brushing aside those individuals who don't fit into a collective vision of the future is troubling, and may actually be serving as a direct antithesis to the mission of social justice at the end of the day.

I'll try to flesh this out more. In some ways, cancel culture is exemplified by our prison system. We send people away to prison after they've committed a crime. It is somewhat implied that the time individuals spend in prison will turn them into good citizens, the kinds of people who don't commit crimes. Yet, over a nine-year time period, released prisoners averaged five arrests. Like cancel culture, the prison system punishes people, but doesn't really provide space for behavioral change. What's more is that the prison population is disproportionately representative of the black and Latinx population in the United States. Obviously there's absolutely no moral equivalence between mass incarceration and the efforts by social justice activists to cancel those responsible for bigoted behaviors or statements, and it's important to recognize that there's a power disparity between the actors in these situations. But for those of us who seek to uphold social justice ideals, it behooves us to think about what it means for one of the mechanisms we access in the name of social justice—cancelling—to so closely resemble a system that produces negative life outcomes disproportionately for people of color.

Engaging in this thought process and envisioning accountability beyond models evocative of oppressive structures are worthwhile exercises if we seek to live out social justice ideals and frameworks. This is not to say that accountability can't, in part, look like cancelling. Sometimes, people commit crimes and engage in behavior so harmful and so galling that they don't deserve a second chance—especially to keep the people around them safe from further harm. But for those who've behaved in ways that can be reasonably unlearned, I believe it's also worth thinking about accountability in terms of restorative justice. In totality, accountability might look like going further than punitive measures to ensure that individuals take active steps to understand the harm they may have perpetuated and develop ways to lead a life in which they've given up harmful notions and tendencies. To do this would be to truly commit ourselves to a socially just society.

> "[Cancel culture is] very toxic but also necessary. We are in the correction phase right now and everyone is indiscriminately calling each other out, and that's because we're working to set new standards and norms as a society."

Cancel Culture Isn't Meant to Be Restorative

Katie Herzog

In the following viewpoint, Katie Herzog argues that the phenomenon of cancel culture is more faceted than many people believe. Calling people out does have its merits, provided our expectations are kept in check. While it's true that the ostracization resulting from being canceled can be extremely damaging, the awareness and cultural norms that emerge from such cancellations can promote social progress. On the other hand, cancel culture cannot do that alone. Ironically, the author found herself targeted by cancel culture after this story was originally published. Katie Herzog is a freelance writer who hosts a podcast, Blocked and Reported.

"Cancel Culture: What Exactly Is This Thing?" by Katie Herzog, The *Stranger*, Index Newspaper LLC, September 17, 2019. Reprinted by permission.

As you read, consider the following questions:

1. Why might cancellation only be effective if it comes from within one's own side?
2. What is the difference between cancellation and critique, according to the viewpoint?
3. According to the author, what is new about cancellation, given that public shaming is not a new phenomenon?

What is cancel culture, and is it improving society or making it worse?

The answer to those questions largely depends on who you ask. Some people, particularly those who consider themselves targets or victims of cancelation campaigns, argue that it is a dangerous trend in American culture, one that is actively stifling art, media, science, education, and free thought. Others argue that cancel culture is just another term for accountability, and that invoking the spectre of cancel culture is just a way of dodging responsibility for one's actions.

But what is cancelation, exactly? There's no one answer to this—the definition, it turns out, is largely in the eye of the beholder—but I think of it as a form of social and cultural boycott. The goal isn't restoration or even analysis; it's excommunication.

I suspect some of the problems with defining the term is that some people think of it as literal and others do not. I'm in the latter camp. Although there are a few notable incidents of people being literally canceled after social media backlash—for instance, Roseanne Barr and James Gunn—I think of "cancelation" as a catchier term for public call-outs, a principle that originated in activist circles to confront wrongdoing in their own communities.

Call-outs began as a utopian ideal, a way of extracting justice and change without cops or courts. But then came the internet. Activist Loretta Ross wrote about this recently in the *New York Times*: "My experiences with call-outs began in the 1970s as a young black feminist activist," she wrote. "I sharply criticized white women for not understanding women of color. I called them out while trying to explain intersectionality and white supremacy." Forty years later, after watching call-outs migrate from in-person to online, Ross has come to the conclusion that this trend isn't just counterproductive but actually toxic.

"Call-outs are justified to challenge provocateurs who deliberately hurt others, or for powerful people beyond our reach," Ross writes. "Effectively criticizing such people is an important tactic for achieving justice. But most public shaming is horizontal and done by those who believe they have greater integrity or more sophisticated analyses. They become the self-appointed guardians of political purity."

The *New York Times* columnist Jamelle Bouie, however, sees the emergence of call-outs and cancelations as a positive development, if not a new one. "There have always been these negotiations in the public sphere about what people can say, and those have always been mediated by who has power and who doesn't," he told me. "What I think is novel about the present is that it's people who, under ordinary circumstances, may not necessarily have power. That, I think, is what's freaking people out—that a bunch of people who, 20 years ago, may have been voiceless all of a sudden have a forum for voicing displeasure and that actually has weight on the institution."

So what is the difference between cancelation and critique? "That's the thing," says Vox senior politics editor Jane Coaston. "I have no idea. Did Roseanne lose her job because of 'cancel culture,' or because she said something stupid and got punished for it? Did *God, The Devil and Bob* get canceled because of 'cancel culture,' or is it only 'cancel culture' when the left is doing it?"

As for how effective cancelation campaigns are, that's debatable, too.

"In internet culture, being canceled is only good for your career," says Taylor Lorenz, a staff writer at the *New York Times* who covers internet culture. "It usually results in going viral, which is default good in today's broken world. It makes your fans stan you harder and it makes more people have an opinion of you, which is usually good because that results in more followers."

Lorenz is talking specifically about Instagram and YouTube influencers, but the same could be said of those in traditional media.

Take *New York Times* columnist Bari Weiss. The outsize and largely negative reaction to her work (and her tweets) is a big part of why she has the massive profile she has now. It's why she's now a regular on Bill Maher (a man who is seemingly immune from being canceled, even after he was literally canceled by ABC) and why people who don't read the *Times* Opinion pages still know who she is.

But even if cancelation can boost your public profile, as in the case of Bari Weiss, notoriety isn't the end-all, be-all of success, and there are real social and emotional downsides to being canceled. This is especially true when it comes from your own tribe.

"Maybe one crucial aspect of canceling is that it only really works if it comes from your own ideological side, maybe even members of your own profession," says essayist Meghan Daum, whose latest book *The Problem with Everything*, touches on this very subject.

"Louis CK's cancelation was led not just by the left but by other comics. Insufficiently woke young adult novelists are canceled by other young adult novelists—or they even self-cancel! Milo Yiannopoulis was finally canceled, but only after his right-wing fans decided his pederasty remarks were a bridge too far. The left couldn't have canceled him, since they already hated him and it would have had no impact."

That, I think, is key. For cancelation to have any impact, it must come from inside the house. This is why Shane Gillis—the comic who *SNL* fired this week after massive outcry after a journalist posted footage of him telling anti-Asian and anti-gay jokes—could be canceled, but Sarah Jeong, the *New York Times* editor with a history of tweeting anti-white jokes, could not. Gillis's critics were fellow comics as well as fans of *SNL*. Jeong's were mostly people who voted for Donald Trump. Who cares what they think?

But cancelation isn't just limited to public figures. Sure, Bari Weiss has far more prominence than she did before people on the internet decided she was trash, but there are other cases in which people who don't have institutional support are rendered unemployable.

Art Tavana, a former columnist at *LA Weekly* and *Playboy* was canceled (for the first time) after writing a column about his obsession with Sky Ferreira (mostly her aesthetic, but there was a line about her body) that generated widespread outrage online, in no small part because the actress herself seemed deeply offended by it. Art was canceled, first metaphorically and then literally when his column was dropped. He still writes—he's working on a book about Guns N Roses—but his income comes from working at an arcade at the mall.

"Being canceled is really no different from being the weird, uncool kid in high school," Tavana told me. "Canceled people tend to be individuals who belong to this weird sort of subgenre, at least those of us in media. There is an aspect to our machinery that is very similar: We're all kind of outsiders and contrarians who are stuck in this weird, homogenized, Instagram monoculture of fake happiness, and we are the bitter, angry, goth people in the corner. We're very alienated, and we're suffering social and economic consequences."

Tavana doesn't seem all that concerned about his own cancelation—he says he never expected to make money writing, so the inability to do so isn't a big shock—but, as he noted, sometimes those who are canceled can end up becoming cancelers themselves.

"I was part of a 'canceled people' text group for a while, and I realized we were exhibiting the same behavior as the people who canceled us," he said. "It was like, 'Oh, f**k these people, let's take them down.' I got disgusted by the group and said I didn't want to be a part of it anymore so I got canceled by the canceled. Or maybe I canceled them."

What Tavana is concerned about it the effect this is having on art, music, and the media, and he's not alone. Heather Heying, the former Evergreen State College professor who, with her husband Bret Weinstein, was targeted by student protesters and later stepped down, calls cancel culture "mob rule."

"People join mobs for a variety of reasons, some of them honorable," Heying says. "Usually those with honorable intentions can't see that it is a mob they are joining. Cancel culture is a bastardization of protest, and of revolution, both of which democratic systems need, but cancel culture seeks to destroy and banish all those who disagree with some new orthodoxy."

That, to Heying, is the difference between cancelation and critique. "Critique involves listening and understanding, and then perhaps trying to change the minds of those who disagree. Instead of trying to change people's minds, the mob removes them from view." This can lead to shunning, not only from strangers, but from colleagues and friends, as Heying and her husband experienced in the aftermath of the scandal at Evergreen.

"It's one of the worst things that can happen to a person, to be ostracized from society," says Meghan Murphy, a Canadian feminist and writer who was permanently banned from Twitter after she misgendered Jessica Yaniv, the now notorious trans woman who filed human rights complaints against female estheticians who refused to wax her [scrotum]. (Perhaps ironically, Yaniv has since been called out herself, both for racism and allegedly sexually harassing minors.)

"Most people join in on the ostracization not because they really understand the 'crime' or believe the canceled individual is truly bad and irredeemable, but because they are following the crowd," Murphy continues. "Either they feel they must, in order to avoid being canceled themselves, or they simply believe second-hand information without investigating the situation themselves."

Others, however, argue that this trend is necessary for social progress.

"Shame and stigma have always been a way to enforce social norms," says James Hamblin, a writer for the *Atlantic* and a cancel-culture skeptic. As an example, he cites homophobia. There was no court ruling or mandate that homophobia is no longer acceptable in society, but Hamblin says that by shaming homophobic viewpoints, they became less acceptable to express, and so society became less homophobic. (I think he's probably right about this to some degree, but large numbers of people coming out to their families and friends might have had more to do with it than simply shaming, and Hamblin agrees.)

To most of us, homophobia is obviously negative and less of it in society is obviously a net good. But one of the problems with cancel culture is that allegations often spread before they're inspected for truth. An accusation is made and instead of waiting for facts to emerge, it's just assumed to be fact.

This appears to be what happened in the case of a Yale Ph.D. student Sarah Braasch, a former international human rights lawyer who worked primarily with African Muslim women in France. In 2018, Braasch became famous after calling the police on a black student who was sleeping in a common area near her dorm room, an incident that became known as "napping while black."

The story of Braasch that spread online was cut and dry: This was a racist woman who called the cops on a black student. The outcry was enormous. Journalist Cathy Young wrote of the aftermath:

> Before long, the deluge of anger had a target with a name and a face. Anti-police violence activist Brittany Packnett, who has more than 200,000 Twitter followers, denounced Braasch as a "danger to black students" and urged Yale to take action; there were calls for her to be not only expelled but criminally charged. Best-selling author Ijeoma Oluo tweeted a de facto call to harassment, suggesting black students should camp out by Braasch's door every night. The fact that the Bigot of the Week was identified as a civil rights activist in her bio on the Yale website was mentioned only as evidence that white allies can be as bad as any white supremacist. "Sarah Braasch even looks like a Nazi," wrote one Twitter leftist.

This story was picked up by the national media, including CNN and the *New York Times*, and anger continued to mount. Braasch ended up fleeing her home, and nearly 3,000 people signed a petition demanding that she be "removed" from campus. While a complaint against her was ultimately withdrawn, she lost her housing, her reputation, and now needs special permission to visit campus.

If Braasch were actually guilty of racism, perhaps social alienation would be a fair price to pay. But when Young investigated this incident a year after it took place, she found that the accusations against Braasch did not stand up to scrutiny. What happened that night was more likely a byproduct of Braasch's documented mental health issues than implicit or explicit bigotry. The truth, as always, is far more complex than the narrative that spread online. Of course, by then it was too late. Despite Young's reporting, there has been little redemption for Braasch.

Braasch may have been a victim of cancel culture gone wrong. But is her case the exception or the rule? Like the definition of cancel culture itself, it depends on who you ask.

"I think the way people use 'cancel culture' is this shorthand way of dismissing whatever accusations are against them," says the *Times'* Taylor Lorenz. "My general take on it is that it's very toxic but also necessary. We are in the correction phase right now and everyone is indiscriminately calling each other out, and that's because we're working to set new standards and norms as a society."

Whether cancel culture is a correction or an over-correction, the impact it is having on people and society is not a myth, says Mike Pesca, host of the *Gist* podcast. "It's real. It tends to get exaggerated by interested parties and downplayed by others, but jobs have been lost, and people have been threatened, and projects have been scrapped. I don't know if it's an epidemic, but there's a chill, and oftentimes that chill is illiberal. That's the big difference between cancelation and critique, I say. Legit critique is liberal, arguing that Dave Chapelle's special was bad or didn't work for specific reasons. Illegitimate critique is illiberal, which is arguing that works shouldn't exist or that arguments shouldn't be made."

One problem with cancel culture is that there is no statute of limitations or mechanism for renewal. "What you've said or done can haunt you for the rest of your life," says Peter Boghossian, the author of just-out book *How to Have Impossible Conversations*. Boghossian is also one of the masterminds behind the "grievance studies hoax," in which he and two others submitted outlandish and entirely made-up studies to academic journals to demonstrate the flaws in these fields of study. (Seven of them were accepted for publication.) In response, 12 of Boghossian's colleagues at Portland State University published an anonymous letter condemning his work and he was later banned from doing human studies research by the college.

"Cultural norms and values are constantly in flux, so you could be punished for a cultural belief you never reflected upon but just took for granted. In the recent past, it was gay marriage; in the near future it may be meat-eating." He calls this trend "a recipe for alienation, loneliness, inauthenticity, and unfairness."

Whatever you call it—public shaming, call-out culture, or cancelation—what's happening now is in no way a new phenomenon. The Dixie Chicks were canceled during the Iraq War for simply saying they were ashamed of George W. Bush. The Hollywood blacklist is another obvious example of cancelation before the term existed.

But what is new is the scale of it all. This isn't just happening to public figures; it's happening everywhere that social media exists, and you no longer have to be powerful, or even notable, to get canceled. And sometimes the offense was committed when the guilty party was just a kid.

"The ubiquity of smart phones means that everybody's statements are permanently recorded—sometimes on video," says Robby Soave, an editor at *Reason* and the author of *Panic Attack: Young Radicals in the Age of Trump*. "Every living person has done or said things they regret, that they would not like to revisit, and wish would just go away. But now, the evidence doesn't just go away. It exists forever. Primarily, this is a problem for kids and teenagers, or people who used to be kids—i.e., everyone!—and are now being held accountable for unwise statements that should have remained in the past."

As for how long this particular moment will last, who knows, but as Meghan Daum told me, "I hope cancel culture keeps expanding and more and more people get canceled, because then eventually everyone will get canceled and it will mean nothing and we'll just have a reset. Cancel culture is inevitably a self-canceling proposition."

> "The idea that someone should be expunged from society for holding controversial ... ideas can have troublesome implications. We are all of us flawed people, and part of living in brotherhood with others involves trying to see the virtues in others."

Tolerance Is More Rewarding Than Cancellation

Fred Bauer

In the following viewpoint, Fred Bauer argues that the wholesale canceling of people harms society in several ways. The author uses the examples of artists throughout history whose views or actions are now considered problematic or downright wrong. Had they been canceled for their beliefs and ideologies, then the world would have missed out on their important societal contributions. The author suggests that we should prioritize tolerance and to seek out the possibilities of others. Fred Bauer is a writer whose work has been featured in numerous publications, including the Weekly Standard *and the* Daily Caller.

"Cancel Culture Impoverishes Both the Heart and the Intellect," by Fred Bauer, *National Review*, September 25, 2019. © 2020 National Review. Used with permission.

As you read, consider the following questions:

1. What is important about how the author distinguishes cancel culture from cultural criticism?
2. What is the Great Awokening, according to the author?
3. When might it be appropriate to cancel someone, according to the viewpoint?

It is trivially—yet essentially—true that all societies have prohibitions; after all, part of what constitutes a society is having prohibitions. But "cancel culture" seems more than just the support of social prohibitions, and the tendencies of this movement might reveal some more-troubling elements.

Because "cancel culture" is an emergent phenomenon, it is hard to create a comprehensive taxonomy of it, but its distinctive elements seem to involve some combination of the following: the destruction of art that either is problematic or whose creators have believed or said something problematic; rendering unemployable those who have believed or said something problematic, especially on social media; the de-platforming of problematic individuals; and participating in a crusade to "cancel" either problematic art or individuals (that is, calling for "cancellation" as cultural participation).

"Cancel culture" is in part about enforcing a set of cultural values (an enterprise not unique to that movement), and it often does so through social-media pressure, which is sometimes aided and abetted by major media institutions. So, for instance, a hubbub starts on Twitter, which CNN then magnifies. It would be naïve to read this as digital democracy; often, major media institutions give a megaphone only to those social-media controversies that they find helpful for their preferred predetermined narrative. For instance, after Halle Bailey was announced as Ariel in a live-action remake of *The Little Mermaid*, major media outlets focused on a few random tweets in order to portray America as a whole as a seething cauldron of racial animosity. Though social media are an important vector for cancel culture, they are often a vehicle rather than a cause.

Cancel culture includes other technological elements, too. Perhaps one of its more distinctive elements is that it occurs during a moment of near-universal legibility. Earlier efforts at ostracism often occurred within discrete localities or subcultures. For Internet-based cancel culture, anyone anywhere can launch an attack on anyone anywhere. Moreover, these attacks are available for all to see over an indefinite period of time. As Helen Andrews has noted, one of the core elements of modern shaming is its endurance. A video clip, a private text message, a Facebook post—anything can be transformed into a cause for public, personal ridicule, which the amber of the Internet preserves across years or even decades. Nor is cancel culture simply about criticizing others on social media. Instead, it is often about translating this

GUILTY BY PUBLIC OPINION

Over the past few weeks, James Charles, a YouTuber in the beauty community, has been a prevalent topic of discussion throughout the internet, from YouTube, Twitter, to even major news sites—specifically the movement to "cancel" him in response to the recent controversy he was involved in. However, the idea of cancel culture confuses me.

All of the drama surrounding Charles began in the middle of April. After posting a video on his Instagram story promoting SugarBear Hair's brand of sleeping vitamins, Tati Westbrook, a YouTuber and collaborator on Charles's channel, responded emotionally in a video on Instagram. Westbrook owns a beauty vitamin company called Halo Beauty, so the fact that Charles promoted a rival company was a probable factor in her response.

On May 10, Westbrook posted a 43-minute video to YouTube expressing frustrations and issues with Charles stemming from the Instagram drama. Within the video, Westbrook accuses Charles of attempting to use his fame and wealth to manipulate straight men into having sexual interactions with him. In addition, Westbrook spoke of a moment when Charles knowingly pursued a straight waiter.

After the internet heard Westbrook's claims, a movement began to "cancel" Charles. In the span of a weekend, Charles lost approximately digital criticism into real personal pain: to cause jobs to be lost, college admissions to be revoked, and media platforms to be shut down. (There's a reason why it's called cancel culture and not criticism culture.)

Cancel culture does not have a single ideological orientation, but, in this present moment, it intertwines with the Great Awokening. Cancel culture is a great tool for evangelical wokeness, in part because of those demographics where wokeness is most concentrated: the college-credentialed meritocrats who reside in major urban areas and function as gatekeepers in tech, major media outlets, educational administration, institutional nonprofits, and so forth. Cancel culture has been a way for the woke to flex their burgeoning muscles as they suppress and splinter dissenters. The suppression part is clear, but this splintering tactic plays a key role; even those who are putatively non-woke have an incentive to go

three million subscribers. Charles was also condemned on a multitude of social media platforms and lost his partnership with Killer Merch.

Since then, he has released a response video revealing that the waiter Westbrook referred to in her video was actually bi-curious at the time, and messaged Charles first.

Personally, I believe that some of Charles's hate has been misguided, and purely the result of a specific type of cancel culture that treats conjecture as fact.

Cancel culture is a complex issue, but fundamentally, cancel culture involves "dumping" or withdrawing from a celebrity or social media influencer who commits an act that social media users deem immoral.

I understand that the idea of cancel culture is meant to give users the power to express their belief on an issue, but I personally can't find the same through line of immorality in this case that is present in other cases.

The idea that the internet would try to cancel an individual purely based on allegations seems hard to justify. When the internet found out about the scandal, it didn't wait for a response from Charles before deeming him guilty in the court of public opinion.

"'Cancel Culture' Should be Cancelled," by Noe Padilla, The Bottom Line, May 23, 2019.

along with some cancellations in order to prove their respectability (that they are not that deplorable). Again, though, the impulses of cancel culture are not confined to the Great Awokening—the "cancellation" of the Dixie Chicks for opposing the Iraq war, for instance, offers a forerunner to contemporary cancel culture (even if the band paid a relatively mild price compared with some of those who endure cancellations today).

Revealingly, opposition to cancel culture reaches across a broad ideological and demographic range. Critics of this movement range from comedian Dave Chappelle to Democratic presidential candidate Andrew Yang to novelist Walter Kirn to polemicist Camille Paglia. It is not too surprising that many of those invested in the arts should be so wary of cancel culture. There may be something philistine about the idea of canceling someone because he holds objectionable opinions. Ezra Pound was a literal Fascist—a man who turned his back on the United States and produced propaganda for Mussolini—and yet his poetry is scintillating; striking it from the libraries of the world would deprive us of some of the gems of poetic modernism. W. E. B. Du Bois's *The Souls of Black Folk* is one of the most penetrating and imaginative surveys of race and identity in the American canon, but he praised Stalin and the USSR. From one perspective, the iron logic of cancel culture leads to gradual intellectual impoverishment, as one figure after another is tossed into the bonfire of the canceled.

And it's hard to shake the feeling that part of what's involved in cancel culture is a breakdown in personal charity. The idea that someone should be expunged from society for holding controversial (or, frankly, even objectionable) ideas can have troublesome implications. We are all of us flawed people, and part of living in brotherhood with others involves trying to see the virtues in others—to not let errors obscure the personhood of another. It is, of course, true that social opprobrium and even state coercion can be instruments for discouraging vice; the first has helped diminish the use of some racial slurs, and the second helps curtail robbery, rape, and murder. But it's also true that stigmatization alone hits diminishing returns in encouraging virtue and that some efforts at stigmatization can be motivated more by atavistic cruelty than by a deep devotion to human dignity.

As with many other issues, talk of "rights" can confuse the question of how to approach cancellation. A legal right to do something doesn't make the action either prudent or virtuous. For instance, members of Congress might have a legal right to denigrate private religious organizations (such as the Knights of Columbus), but it's not clear that such behavior serves the interests of American pluralism or good government. Someone might have a legal right to denigrate the poor and suffering, but such a display would offer anything but an edifying example. Likewise, the teeming crowds on social media might have a legal right to call for someone to be fired, for a book to be expunged by its publisher, or for a work of art to be destroyed. A tireless agitation for the personal destruction of others might, however, corrode both personal lives and public norms.

Within some opposition to cancel culture, it's possible to see an impulse toward openness, expansion, and pluralism. For this countervailing impulse, another person's problematic trait doesn't mean that he or she has nothing valuable to contribute to one's own life and to society as a whole. You might not want a flat-earther as a geological adviser—but why not as a carpenter, a neighbor, or a comedian? A Christian might read Homer despite his polytheism, a liberal might read Pound despite his fascism, and a humanitarian might read Du Bois despite his Soviet sympathies. The point is not to destroy impure people but instead to see virtues in this mottled world.

From this pluralist perspective, there might indeed be times where some form of "cancellation" is appropriate. For instance, college students might protest if their institution paid for a literal neo-Nazi to be a commencement speaker. Different institutions would, of course, be able to formulate their own internal norms, but one might make a case for at least some institutions to have a place for some kind of pluralism. Politics might complicate some of this. Citizens have a right and even a duty to deliberate on those norms that will guide a government, so some level of "cancellation" might be inherent in any politics. But taking this pluralist approach, we would turn to cancellation as an emergency measure, not a standard practice.

Crucial to maintaining a free society is disciplining both the power of government and the power of individuals. A government without internal balances can soon degenerate into tyranny or anarchy; a citizenry who do not show the virtues necessary for sustaining a republic will soon undermine the foundations of liberty. Maintaining norms of tolerance involves some modes of discipline—to see beyond outrage, to grasp the possibilities of others, and to recognize one's own limits. That discipline might bring great rewards, too. The bonfire of the canceled casts a far dimmer glow than the raw flames of charity, beauty, and cultural daring.

Periodical and Internet Sources Bibliography

The following articles have been selected to supplement the diverse views presented in this chapter.

Dalin Brown, "Twitter's Cancel Culture: A Force for Good or a Digital Witchhunt? The Answer Is Complicated," *USA Today*, July 17, 2020. https://www.usatoday.com/story/tech/2020/07/17/has -twitters-cancel-culture-gone-too-far/5445804002/

Maria Coole, "Why Cancel Culture Needs to Be Cancelled," *Marie Claire*, January 22, 2020. https://www.marieclaire.co.uk/opinion /cancel-culture-682272

Tyler Cowen, "No, America Will Not Be Canceled," Bloomberg, September 1, 2020. https://www.bloomberg.com/opinion /articles/2020-09-01/-cancel-culture-will-not-take-over -america-fortnite-will

Daniel Dale, "A List of People and Things Donald Trump Tried to Get Canceled Before He Railed Against Cancel Culture," CNN, July 7, 2020. https://www.cnn.com/2020/07/07/politics/fact-check -trump-cancel-culture-boycotts-firings/index.html

George Leef, "College Campuses Gave Us Cancel Culture," *National Review*, November 2, 2020. https://www.nationalreview.com /corner/college-campuses-gave-us-cancel-culture/

Roy Meredith, "Ending Cancel Culture Is Up to You," New Discourses, June 24, 2020. https://newdiscourses.com/2020/06 /ending-cancel-culture/

NPR, "What We Talk About When We Talk About 'Cancel Culture,'" July 20, 2020. https://www.npr.org/2020/07/20/893034155/what -we-talk-about-when-we-talk-about-cancel-culture

Osita Nwanevu, "The 'Cancel Culture' Con," *New Republic*, September 23, 2019. https://newrepublic.com/article/155141/cancel-culture -con-dave-chappelle-shane-gillis

Noe Padilla, "Cancel Culture Should Be Cancelled," The Bottom Line, May 23, 2019. https://thebottomline.as.ucsb.edu/2019/05/cancel -culture-should-be-cancelled

Emma Rosemurgey, "It's Time to Leave Toxic Cancel Culture in 2019," UNILAD, January 8, 2020. https://www.unilad.co.uk /featured/its-time-to-leave-toxic-cancel-culture-in-2019/

Tim Stanley, "Cancel Culture Will Fizzle Out—As These Lessons from History Prove," *Telegraph*, September 19, 2020. https://www .telegraph.co.uk/art/what-to-see/think-cancel-culture-millennial -wrong-vindictive-erasure-harks/

Joel Stein, "The Day Cancel Culture Was Canceled," *LA Magazine*, February 14, 2020. https://www.lamag.com/citythinkblog/cancel -culture-canceled/

Thinkhouse, "Post-Cancel Culture: Coronavirus & 'Canceled' 2.0," retrieved September 17, 2020. https://www.thinkhousehq.com /insights/post-cancel-culture-coronavirus-cancelled-2-0

For Further Discussion

Chapter 1

1. After reading chapter 1, would you define cancel culture as a good or bad movement? Defend your position using examples from the viewpoints in this chapter.
2. How would you define cancel culture? Does it exist only online or does it occur in day-to-day existence, too?
3. Do you feel cancel culture is a new phenomenon or has it been with us in some form or another through history?

Chapter 2

1. What do you believe is the most harmful effect of cancel culture? How does it affect everyday people?
2. Are there ever positive or good outcomes from cancel culture? Provide examples.
3. What is hashtag activism? Think of situations where hashtag activism has achieved positive results and those in which it has veered into the negative actions.

Chapter 3

1. What positive contributions did the hashtag activism in #MeToo perform for society? Did it cause any negative repercussions?
2. Should some public people whose speech and actions are so reprehensible indeed be canceled? Why or why not?
3. Why do you think former president Barack Obama has won wide bipartisan approval for his take on cancel culture?

Chapter 4

1. Do you think cancel culture will ever be canceled completely from society?
2. How has cancel culture been addressed in US politics? Does the conservative right have a different take on cancel culture than the liberal left?
3. Is cancel culture just another tech form of vigilantism, or is it something more?

Organizations to Contact

The editors have compiled the following list of organizations concerned with the issues debated in this book. The descriptions are derived from materials provided by the organizations. All have publications or information available for interested readers. The list was compiled on the date of publication of the present volume; the information provided here may change. Be aware that many organizations take several weeks or longer to respond to inquiries, so allow as much time as possible.

American Civil Liberties Union

125 Broad Street, 18th Floor
New York, NY 10004
(212) 549-2500
website: www.aclu.org

The American Civil Liberties Union (ACLU) is the premier defender of the rights enshrined in the US Constitution. With a vast network of attorneys, the ACLU fights government abuse and defends individual freedoms, including speech and religion.

Center for Democracy and Technology

Tower Building
1401 K Street NW, Suite 200
Washington, DC 20005
(202) 637-9800
website: www.cdt.org

The Center for Democracy and Technology, founded in 1994, works to define, promote, and influence technology policy and the internet by strengthening individual human rights and freedoms. It is based in Washington, DC.

Courage Foundation

email: courage.contact@couragefound.org
website: www.couragefound.org

The Courage Foundation is an international organization that supports whistleblowers and others who risk their lives of liberty to make significant contributions by mounting defenses for these individuals and forcing their cases into the public sphere. Clients include Julian Assange of Wikileaks. It was founded in 2013.

Cyberbullying Report

website: cyberbullyingreport.com

A members-only portal, the Cyberbullying Report hopes to make the internet a safer place, empowering victims of online harassment to fight back online.

The Cybersmile Foundation

US West Office
530 Lytton Avenue, 2nd Floor
Palo Alto, CA 94301
email: info@cybersmile.org
website: www.cybersmile.org

The Cybersmile Foundation is a nonprofit dedicated to tackling all forms of bullying and abuse online, working to promote kindness, diversity, and inclusion. It was founded in 2010.

Electronic Frontier Foundation

815 Eddy Street
San Francisco, CA 94109
(415) 436-9333
email: info@eff.org
website: www.eff.org

Electronic Frontier Foundation (EFF) is a nonprofit civil liberties group that advocates for First Amendment rights in the area of digital and other new technologies.

Facebook

1 Hacker Way
Menlo Park, CA 94025
(650) 308-7300
website: www.Facebook.com

Currently one of the leading social networks in the world, Facebook was started in 2004 for college students by CEO Mark Zuckerberg. It went public in 2012.

Family Online Safety Institute

1440 G Street NW
Washington, DC 2005
(202) 775-0158
email: press@fosi.org
website: www.fosi.org

FOSI works internationally to provide a safer digital world for kids and their families, promoting a culture of responsibility online. It was founded in 2007.

Fed Up with Cancel Culture

Facebook Group
website: www.Facebook.com

Fed Up with Cancel Culture is a right-leaning Facebook interest group dedicated to discussing instances of cancel culture nationwide.

First Amendment Coalition

534 Fourth Street, Suite B
San Rafael, CA 94901
(415) 460-5060
email: fac@firstamendmentcoalition.org
website: https://firstamendmentcoalition.org/about/

The First Amendment Coalition is an award-winning nonprofit public interest organization dedicated to advancing free speech, more open and accountable government, and public participation in civic affairs.

Freedom House

1850 M Street NW
11th Floor
Washington, DC 20036
(202) 296-5101
email: info@freedomhouse.org
website: www.freedomhouse.org

Freedom House is an independent watchdog organization dedicated to the expansion of freedom and democracy around the world. Freedom House is notable for its nonpartisan character and commitment to maintaining support for its mission among members of both major US political parties.

Get Safe Online

website: www.getsafeonline.org

Get Safe Online promotes unbiased, factual, and easy to understand online safety information, partnering with the public and private sector, including the Microsoft Corporation.

Institute for Free Speech

1150 Connecticut Avenue NW
Suite 801
Washington, DC 20036
website: www.ifs.org

The Institute for Free Speech promotes and defends the First Amendment rights to freely speak, assemble, publish, and petition the government through strategic litigation, communication, activism, training, research, and education.

John Locke Foundation

4800 Six Forks Road
Suite 220
Raleigh, NC 27609
(919) 828-3876
email: info@johnlocke.org
website: www.johnlocke.org

The John Locke Foundation was founded in 1990 as a thinktank and research institute in North Carolina and named for the English philosopher John Locke. It has written and done research on cancel culture from a legal perspective.

Kind Campaign

email: admin@kindcampaign.com
website: www.kindcampaign.com

Kind Campaign is an internationally recognized nonprofit organization that builds awareness of and support for girl-on-girl bullying through assessment, education, and its documentary film.

National Coalition Against Censorship

19 Fulton Street, Suite 407
New York, NY 10038
(212) 807-6222
email: ncac@ncac.org
website: https://ncac.org/free-expression-network

National Coalition Against Censorship (NCAC) is a coalition of over 50 national nonprofit organizations. They work to promote freedom of thought, inquiry, and expression and oppose censorship in all its forms.

Pacer's National Bullying Prevention Center

8161 Normandale Boulevard
Minneapolis, MN 55437
email: bullying411@Pacer.org
website: www.pacer.org

Pacer's National Bullying Prevention Center was founded in 2006 and actively seeks to end childhood bullying in schools, in communities, and online.

Pew Research Center

1615 L Street NW, Suite 800
Washington, DC 20036
(202) 419-4300
website: www.pewresearch.org

Based in Washington, DC, the Pew Research Center is a nonpartisan foundation offering data-driven social science research. It was established in 2004 by founder Andrew Kohut.

Southern Poverty Law Center

400 Washington Avenue
Montgomery, AL 36104
(888) 414-7752
website: www.splcenter.org

The Southern Poverty Law Center monitors hate groups and extremists, publishes investigative reports, teaches tolerance, and offers expert analysis to the media and public.

Stomp Out Bullying

220 East 57th Street, 9th Floor
New York, NY 10022-2805
(877) 602-8559
website: www.stompoutbullying.org

Stomp Out Bullying works to reduce and prevent bullying, cyberbullying, and other digital abuse; educates against homophobia, LGBTQ+ discrimination, racism, and hatred; and deters violence in schools, online, and in communities across the country.

StopBullying

US Department of Health and Human Services
200 Independence Avenue SW
Washington, DC 20201
website: www.stopbullying.gov

StopBullying is a federal government website managed by the US Department of Health and Human Services that offers information from a variety of governmental agencies concerning bullying, cyberbullying, prevention, and response.

Twitter

1355 Market #900
San Francisco, CA 94103
(415) 222-9670
website: www.twitter.com

Twitter is a social network information portal originally intended to share information quickly in a small space—in 140 characters or less. Twitter claims more than 500 million tweets daily.

WikiLeaks

www.wikileaks.org

WikiLeaks, founded by Julian Assange in 2006, is a multi-national media organization with a library dedicated to censored or otherwise restricted official material involving war, espionage, and corruption.

Bibliography of Books

Meghan Daum. *The Problem with Everything: My Journey Through the New Culture Wars*. New York, NY: Gallery Books, 2019.

Thomas Frank. *Listen Liberal*. New York, NY: Metropolitan Books, 2016.

Tammy Gagne. *Online Shaming and Bullying*. San Diego, CA: Reference Point Press, 2019.

Tracy Brown Hamilton. *Combatting Internet Shaming*. New York, NY: Rosen Publishing Group, Inc., 2016.

Laurie Helgoe. *Fragile Bully: Understanding Our Destructive Affair with Narcissism in the Age of Trump*. New York, NY: Diversion Books, 2019.

Robert M. Henderson. *Social Media Shaming and Bullying*. San Diego, CA: Reference Point Press, 2020.

Penelope Holt and Samuel Kronen, editors. *Dissenters Project: The Price of Honest Dissent in Cancel Culture*. Dissenters Press, 2019.

Jennifer Jaquet. *Is Shaming Necessary? New Uses for an Old Tool*. New York, NY: Knopf Doubleday, 2015.

Douglas Murray. *The Madness of Crowds: Gender, Race and Identity*. New York, NY: Bloomsbury Continuum, 2019.

Suzanne Nossel. *Dare to Speak: Defending Free Speech for All*. New York, NY: Dey Street Books, 2020.

Tamra B. Orr. *I Have Been Shamed on the Internet, Now What?* New York, NY: Rosen Publishing Group, 2016.

Julian Petley. *Media and Public Shaming: Drawing the Boundaries of Disclosure*. London, UK: I.B. Taurist Company, LTD.

Michael Rectenwald. *Beyond Woke.* Nashville, TN: New English Review Press, 2020.

Jon Ronson. *So You Have Been Publicly Shamed.* New York, NY: Riverhead, 2015.

Sue Scheff. *Shame Nation: The Global Epidemic of Online Hate.* Napier, IL: Sourcebook, 2017.

Mari Swingle. *How and Why Constant Connectivity Is Rewiring Our Brains and What to Do About It.* Gabriola Island, BC, Canada: New Society Publishers, 2019.

Index